Make Money, Save Money, Feel Good

Master the skills required to sell quantified and differentiated value in today's economy

Effective selling involves asking a customer, who either is or you hope will become your friend, a question, giving them the courtesy of listening to their answer, probing to fully understand their needs, offering them a solution that meets these and asking them to buy it from you.

MIKE BRERETON

Title: Make Money, Save Money, Feel Good
Author: Mike Brereton
Copyright: 2021 by Mike Brereton

ISBN: 978-1-953606-06-8

Contents

The Sales Process

People move into sales careers for a variety of reasons and at a variety of stages in their lives and careers. Therefore, inevitably their starting point, perspectives, motivators, and drivers are different.

We are also individuals, with our own way of approaching situations, handling the people we interact with either as colleagues or customers, and conducting our role as salespeople.

Regardless, our main objective in our respective roles is to deliver profitable customer orders to our business and this is ultimately how our effectiveness as a salesperson will be judged.

Therefore, if there were a way in which we could be more effective at this primary function and enhance our enjoyment of it, then why wouldn't we try this?

What you will learn from this book is an approach that has been developed and enhanced during a thirty-year career in sales and sales leadership. It builds upon solid practices established and refined over decades, draws from approaches such as solution, needs fulfilment, challenger, insight, consultant, and numerous other sales practices. The approach has been used successfully by hundreds of salespeople with varying backgrounds and cultures, selling a wide variety of products, services, and solutions into numerous end-markets across multiple geographies and at all levels of customer contacts.

It will provide you with a consistent, repeatable approach that you can customise to make your own while enabling you to manage the multiple challenges, interruptions and diversions that will, invariably, come your way.

If you put the effort in to understand its rationale, absorb, practise, and enhance it, I have no doubt that you, your team, colleagues, and family will benefit from it. Your self-confidence will be enhanced, as will your happiness, reputation, career, and income.

This process has and will continue to evolve as the business world adapts to changes such as reduced customer personnel, increased automation, more readily available product information, changing decision making processes, Industry 4.0 (Internet of Things, Artificial Intelligence) and of course the impact of the global coronavirus pandemic.

It is intended to provide you with a path to follow, not a word-by-word script for you to implement blindly. You will need to make it your own and put some effort into practising aspects of this, which will initially be a little unfamiliar, or even uncomfortable.

A Career In Sales

Many salespeople develop lifelong careers in sales with significant variations in their levels of success, depending on the many ways it could be expressed. To provide you with a form of comparison, shown below is my interpretation of levels of success in a sales career compared with equivalent careers or roles. This, intentionally, does not take into consideration geographic or sector variations but is intended to provide a 'rough' guide for consideration.

LEVEL OF SALES SUCCESS	EQUIVALENT
Moderate	Artisan, technician, junior manager
Good	Senior departmental manager
High Performer	Professional such as accountant or lawyer
Exceptional	Internationally operating business executive, successful entrepreneur

To be clear, what I am intending by this is to show, for example, that an individual who has achieved what I describe as a 'good' level of success in sales, will probably have an income level equivalent to a senior manager in a typical successful business. They will likely own their own home in a desirable neighbourhood, have two cars, take a couple of good holidays each year, pay for two or more children's education and be able to eat out at good quality restaurants several times a month.

The above, may not be how anyone chooses to spend their money of course, but hopefully it puts 'success' into context.

The process, explanations and ideas I share in this book are intended to enable you to, as a minimum, achieve the 'good' level as I describe it and will equip you to progress much further, if that is what you desire.

My Career In Sales

I embarked on my sales career, after having been an engineer with the British Royal Navy for 14 years, at the age of 30. This was at a later age and career stage than many do. As a result of good training, supportive managers, an excellent sales coach and hard work, I was able to progress after two years in field sales, to a sales manager role, then to own my own sales and distribution company for seven years before moving into a variety of general management, consulting and senior sales leadership roles with multi-national corporations. Throughout this time, in each of these roles, I remained actively involved in all aspects of selling, account development and relationship building.

I achieved significant levels of income growth and enjoyed the material wealth in line with the 'exceptional' description above. This came as a result of hard work, application, tenacity, resilience in the face of setbacks, of which there were several, and good fortune. Throughout the thirty years of this career I was continually learning, developing, applying and refining the various methods and techniques outlined in this book. I also had tremendous fun, travelled the world, and worked with some great people who all, in some way, contributed to my success.

Therefore, whether you are new into sales or have been selling for many years, there will be something in this book for you. Even if your main job isn't selling, but you get involved with customers by helping to frame or design a solution as an engineer, consultant, service provider or any other customer facing role, this book will enlighten, stimulate and inform you how to be more effective.

Fundamentally, the approach I share here works, this I know to be true.

Let us get started.

Mike Brereton
Author, Salesperson, Sales Leader, Coach and Mentor

CHAPTER ONE

Objectives of the Book for its Readers

During Reading

1. Introduce a structured sales process to readers and provide them with opportunities to customise it to their situation.

2. Introduce the competency of Curious Investigation, explain its relevance and applicability to sales and suggest methodologies to enhance this.

3. Instil readers with a desire to enthusiastically put the process and tools introduced and explained into use in their daily selling activities.

Within Three-Months of Reading

1. Develop and enhance through practise a structured, consistent sales methodology

2. Improve your opportunity conversion rate, however they may be generated, and increase your sales.

3. Understand how you can better utilise all existing business tools and processes such as your CRM and quote generator/configurator to gain personal and collective benefit from them.

4. Enjoy your sales role more as a result of feeling more confident in every sales situation and increasing your earnings.

One Year After Reading

1. Remain stimulated and equipped to meet and exceed your sales objectives or targets consistently.

2. Produce improved standards of personal performance and income for the remainder of your career in sales.

3. Share with enthusiasm your sales skills and love of sales as a career.

Practise, practise, practise.

CHAPTER TWO

Format of this Book

This is intended to be a 'self-help' book and throughout you will find a series of exercises that aim to get you thinking around the specific aspect of the sales process being focused on. After each exercise we have included relevant ideas and suggestions to supplement your own thoughts, so that you are benefitting from the collective experiences of many successful salespeople as you progress.

You will find a combination of written materials, visual representations and self-developmental exercises that should be relevant to all readers, regardless of their sales experience, products or services sold, geographic location, markets, sectors, gender, and culture.

It will provide opportunities for you to reflect and engage in stimulating thought while reviewing at a pace that suits you.

We will achieve this by:

- Sharing or introducing ideas and concepts
- Providing explanations
- Using 'real-world' examples to illustrate specific points
- Having you engage in multiple self-developmental exercises
- Encouraging reflective self-evaluation

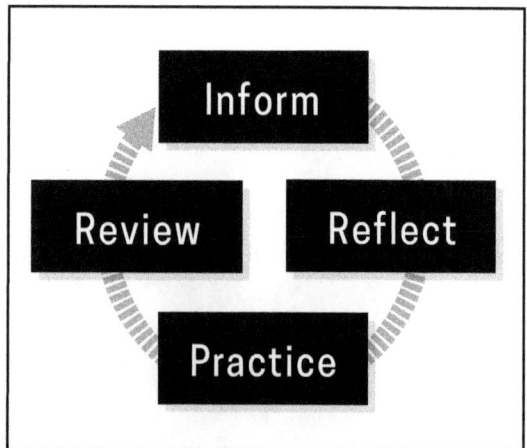

Inform

Reflect

Practice

Review

CHAPTER THREE

Personal Objectives

The fact that you are reading this book indicates you are interested in developing your sales skills, and therefore yourself in general.

Soon after starting to run my own sales and distribution business, which sold fluid handling equipment into a variety of industries, I established an objective to win an account, to whom we initially had some limited sales, from a competitor who was supplying the vast majority of their requirements. The customer designed, manufactured and sold fluid handling systems into the semi-conductor industry and, at the time, was one of the largest of its type in Europe and was privately owned.

I wrote the objective down, put a timeframe of twelve-months on it, quantified how much sales I believed it could bring and included the profitability goal within this too. I shared the objective with the salesperson who had the day-to-day responsibility for account, the manufacturer whose products I distributed and, in this instance, the owner of the customer too.

Within nine-months we had turned the account to us and it became our major customer over the remaining years I owned and operated the business. There was a detailed plan associated with the objective and undoubtedly a key element was the need to establish a good personal relationship with the business owner as well as continue to demonstrate the business benefits to them of having us as their key supplier.

Documenting objectives, sharing them appropriately and working through the plan necessary to achieve them is therefore good practice, as the above example illustrates.

You might already have personal and professional objectives, and these will no doubt have some time element associated with them. Equally, maybe you either do not have any, or have not chosen to write these down.

Regardless, let us establish and record some objectives, either in this book directly or somewhere else that you can refer to later. The two perspectives we're suggesting for the time-framed objectives are; firstly, what would you like to gain from this book as a result of reading it, secondly, what would you like to be able to achieve within three-months of completing it and finally one year after reading it.

Let us use the SMART format to establish these objectives for you

a. On completion of reading

b. Three months after reading

c. One year after reading

A SMART Objective is:

S   **Specific**, well defined, and clear to understand

M   **Measurable** results to ensure you know whether the goal was achieved

A   **Attainable** results given the availability of resources, information, and time

R   **Relevant** to the situation you are in and any larger, longer-term goal you are trying to achieve

T   **Time-based** with clarity over what period you are trying to achieve this goal

CHAPTER FOUR

A Structured Sales Process – Introduction and Overview

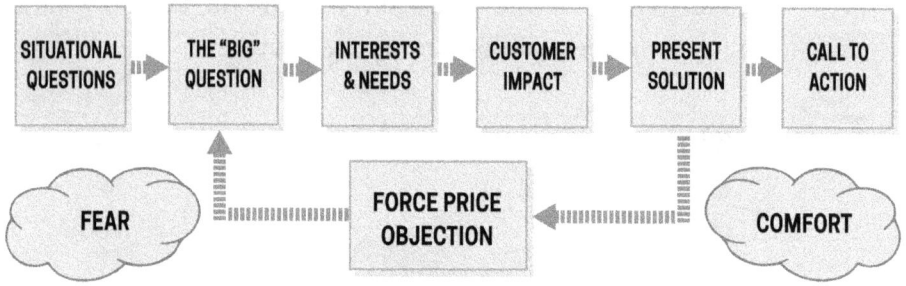

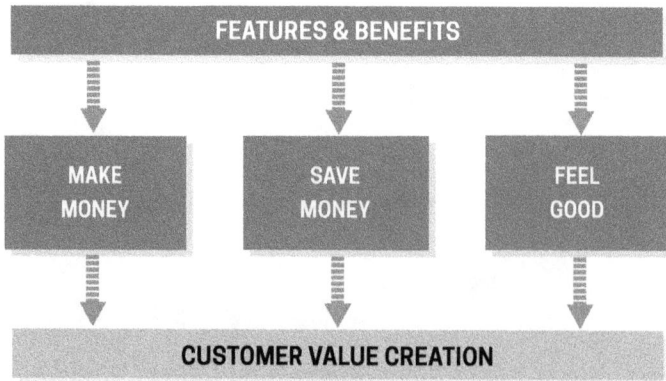

A Structured Sales Process - Overview

O ver the next few pages we'll provide you with an overview of this so that you can visualise how each element fits together to become a process. As you progress further in the book, you will find more detailed reviews and explanations of these elements.

We will review how to approach securing a meeting and preparing for it in the next section, so for now, I'd like you to imagine you're meeting face to face with a customer, either for the first time or someone who you have met with previously.

We will walk through this using the top third of the drawing as a guide moving left to right, dropping down to the centre, and bottom third, periodically.

You will note the 'Fear' and 'Comfort' labels. These are the typical emotions we feel at these stages, particularly when initially engaging in this sales approach.

The great majority of salespeople are most at ease when discussing their product or service as they are familiar with this and like to share information relating to it with their customers—hence the 'Comfort' label. We understand how you can feel in some way 'pressured' by the customer, even though you may not actually be so, to give them information and show them how much you know about your product or service.

However, how can we be sure that what we are sharing with the customer is truly relevant to them at that particular time? Their circumstances, preferences and priorities may change at any time, including perhaps since we last met them. It therefore makes sense and is respectful, to ensure we verify or understand this at the start of our discussions.

We do this by asking a series of questions to enhance our understanding of *their* situation, *current* needs and factors that will affect any decisions related to the potential use of our products or service. This stage is frequently the one which salespeople spend the least time in and are therefore, understandably, 'Fearful' of this.

The most important question of all, though certainly not the only question which is required, we describe as '**The Big Question**". This is always basically the same question, regardless of your product and service or situation and we modify it accordingly:

"Mr. Customer, when you design/specify/select/install/upgrade/ maintain/replace your........., what are the things/factors you take into consideration to help you choose which option/technology/ supplier you will use?"

When they respond, they are sharing with you their **Interests** and **Needs**, in this book we abbreviate these to **IN**s, which can generally be categorised or thought about under the headings of the **Big Four**:

Product & Service	describes something about what this should do for them
Logistics	how, where and when they may need the product or service
Commercial	includes but not limited to, budget constraints, payment terms, price
Personalised Service	generally describes something extremely specific that typically only a human being can offer or is needed to develop for them

Once these have been agreed and verified, we proceed to probe with further questions in order to understand their priorities and the impact of these either being met or not. This impact should be quantified in either Operational Impact, e.g. enhanced production rate/capacity or Financial Impact, e.g. product loss reductions or saved labour-hours.

Once we have identified this, only then should we offer a solution that meets these requirements and move into the phase where most salespeople typically have more 'Comfort' by speaking about and presenting our relevant solution in the form of a product or service.

When we present our solution, we need to fully understand our own product portfolio in order to highlight the specific **Features** which we define as:

something we can typically see or touch

link this to the Benefit that answers the (potentially unasked but always relevant) question of the customer:

"what does this do for me"

or

"what's in it for me?"

and further explain the impact of this in the form of how this helps the customer do one, or a combination of, all three of the following:

Make Money	e.g. sell their product or service at a higher price due to improved specification
Save Money	e.g. reduce the cost of business operations, production, or maintenance
Feel Good	e.g. take work off their desk, enhance safe operations, improve their personal reputation etc.

These elements will form the basis of your **Differentiating Value Proposition or Statement** and will be the compelling reason for your customer to select your solution.

You will note the 'feedback' loop labelled: **"Force The Price Objection"**.

This loop is there as we encourage a healthy discussion about commercial elements (price) at this stage to ensure there is alignment of understanding and matched expectations between you and your customer of what your solution is, how much this is likely to cost, and what the positive impact for them will be of selecting it.

In other words, rarely do professional buyers make a decision without knowing what they will need to pay. A professional salesperson should anticipate this and be an expert at discussing it. So even if a potential customer has not asked the 'how much' question, we suggest you do the following to 'force the price objection'.

Using appropriate wording check that these expectations are aligned:

e.g. "...this solution will be in the range of...$/£/€ XXX., how does that align with your expectations?"

There will never be a better opportunity to re-affirm the relevant **INs**, provide a link via the **Features** & **Benefits** to the **Make Money, Save Money** and/or **Feel Good** statements than after this structured approach. We will explore this further later.

When the customer indicates this is all of interest, accepts these benefits and price point then we naturally progress, or transition, into the phase when we would expect to begin to finalise and secure a commitment to order/specify our proposed solution – i.e. we 'Close'.

Assuming there is agreement to do this, we then agree the next steps you and your customer will take and clearly formalise who will do what, and by when, to ensure there is full alignment and understanding.

Depending on the circumstances, the above process could take under an hour or possibly several days, weeks, months or even years. It is fundamentally the same process, regardless of it's duration, that can be moved away from for a variety of reasons where necessary and re-entered at any stage over a period of time.

We are going to examine this even further and explore each element in more detail as we progress.

CHAPTER FIVE

Securing Face-to-Face Meetings with Customers

This can be the most challenging aspect of a sales role. Particularly in the early stages of a career in sales, or when moving to a new company or sales territory, when you may no longer have a set of customer contacts that you can work with. It can, for many salespeople, present a significant enough challenge as a result of the multiple rejections they receive, for them to become disillusioned enough to choose to leave sales altogether.

I remember, very clearly, how challenging gaining appointments for face to face meetings was during the first two to three months of my own sales career. I was full of enthusiasm, energy, newly learned product knowledge and couldn't wait to share this and meet customers.

Yet, despite having been given some customer accounts, prior purchase records and some guidance from managers it was a real struggle to even speak with prospective contacts on the phone. When I did manage to do so, it seemed they were aware of the products I had to offer, had either ceased using them as they had found alternatives, or couldn't think when they might consider using them again, and were not interested in meeting with me.

There was an expectation from my managers that I would make five confirmed appointments per day and actually achieve eight face-to-face meetings daily, by adding at least three cold-calls to these appointments.

I would spend all day on Fridays trying to set up these meetings for the following week and was required to submit a 'call plan' over the weekend. This would be reviewed by my managers on Monday mornings and voicemails, with 'feedback', left accordingly. The enjoyment of my weekends was in direct proportion to how many appointments I had managed to make for the following week.

I eventually managed to improve the situation, and was able to achieve the necessary call-rates while 'only' requiring a half-day intense phone calling to achieve this. Though I clearly remember that the very first appointment I secured resulted in a 'no show' by the customer and a very demoralised 'bright and shiny new salesman' returning, despondently, to his car!

Therefore, the ideas we will share with you in this section are based on real-life experiences and consolidate many great ideas from multiple salespeople who have all faced, and overcome, such challenges.

The most important principle to remember when trying to secure a meeting is that there has to be some tangible benefit for the customer or prospective customer of agreeing to meet with you.

We recently worked with a large industrial and commercial refrigeration equipment and services provider, whose newly recruited salesperson with over twenty-years 'moderate' sales experience, when phoning to try and establish a face-to-face meeting with customers, would suggest:

"Getting together for a coffee and a catch up."

We explained that if these customers had any sense of priority, influence, or seniority in their businesses, it was highly unlikely they would agree to dedicate some of their valuable time for such a reason. As mentioned above, we explained the necessity to ensure there is a valid reason and benefit **to the customer** to commit to a visit. Ensure you provide this reason/benefit in your rationale for a meeting.

Therefore, we are including in this section, some ideas that we know have worked for many salespeople and will provide some ideas to consider.

There is no doubt that in recent years, with the general reduction in employees, as a result of efficiency improvements and adoption of technology, securing these meetings with customers has become more challenging. Bearing this in mind, there are two key factors for us to consider:

1. **A customer will need to understand the benefit to them of agreeing to give up some of their time to meet with you.**

2. **You will need to ensure that you maximise the effectiveness of your time with them and, if possible, secure future meetings before you leave them.**

Let us consider the first of these.

It may take some time for you to get their phone number and then be able to speak to them, so when you do it is vital that you establish, quickly and succinctly, what the benefit to them of agreeing to meet you is. Therefore, here are some basic ideas of statements you could make. These, as usual, will need amending to suit your and the customer's situation:

> *"We worked recently with your colleague (insert their name) and they were very happy with what we were able to provide for them (insert relevant information). As a result, they suggested I reached out to you as they believe you would be interested in this (insert brief description) too. When would be a good time for us to meet so that I can briefly share how we have added value to them and see how we might do the same for you?"*

> *"We have worked with a number of people in what we understand to be similar companies/roles/situations as yours and we've been able to significantly positively impact their operations/profitability/situations. I only need a few minutes of your time to share with you how we've been able to achieve this, when would be a good time for us to meet?"*

> *"As a result of the changes in (insert relevant industry standard, code or practice) we have developed some new solutions related to (insert situation you believe they will be familiar with) and we firmly believe we can enhance your operations/situation too. I only need a few minutes of your time to share with you how we've been able to achieve this, when would be a good time for us to meet?"*

> *"It's been some time since we met (or since you met with someone from my company) and we have made some significant developments since then (new products, technologies, applications). When would be a good time for us to meet so that I can briefly share some of these with you and help you identify how we can add further value to you?"*

Note, the stated intent is for any meeting they agree to will be brief, therefore not taking too much of their time, identifies there will be something of value to them, and provides a level of justification or reference to your credibility.

All of the above are improvements on the "coffee and a catch up" approach.

Following the structured sales approach, we describe in this book, will ensure you consistently address the second consideration we outlined above, that of ensuring you do not waste the customer's time. If you can secure follow-up meetings, and/or obtain referrals, on conclusion of your meeting you will save significant amounts of time with seemingly endless chasing and reduce the frustration of not being able to expand your contact base.

Contact-Generating Campaigns

There are many ways in which you could obtain a contact name, you can find their details via company website reviews or via searches on LinkedIn or other.

If you are trying to accomplish this without additional support from either others within your company or an external provider, then reviewing a potential or existing customer's website, within their 'who's who' section, could enable you to find this.

LinkedIn searches can also be fruitful and enable you to uncover significant details about a potential contact, though this will depend on the information they choose to make public. LinkedIn offer training on how to conduct these searches and we recommend undertaking this prior to embarking on an extensive search process as this will be time, and money, well spent.

Your company may run campaigns focused on the relevant sectors and geographies or they could choose to work with a company that provides this type of campaign. These approaches typically seek to engage a targeted group of potential contacts by emailing a link to a relevant white paper or article, and encouraging them to 'click-through' in order to access this.

Some campaigns will extend this to enable the contacts to attend a webinar or forum and in so doing generate qualified leads that can subsequently be followed up by salespeople. There are varying levels of success with these campaigns but have been reported as high as 8% of targeted contacts resulting in an engagement with a salesperson. This compares with under 4% for other pure email campaigns.

As an illustration, one such campaign carried out by a company that specialises in this task for other companies, had a contact database of over 300,000 individuals in decision making roles within a particular sector. Of these, 8,500 were in roles believed to be relevant for this specific campaign and were targeted by email inviting a 'click-through' to read a topic specific white paper. Of these, around 100 downloaded the paper and 50 attended a webinar, with 35 of these agreeing to contribute to a forum. While all of the contacts provided relevant details including their phone number, those attending the forum were classed as 'A' category contacts and these were then approached by salespeople to secure a face to face appointment. The others were identified as either 'B' or 'C' category contacts and were telephone by the company's internal sales teams to establish their situation and potential interest in the company's products and services.

A process such as the above can take between six and twelve months and, as can be determined from a review of the headline data, requires careful planning and execution.

The key message used in these campaigns should focus on the value generated, or problem solved, as described in the white paper or article, rather than a message about the potential product or service, as messages with this as the focus have been shown to be less successful.

Hints and Tips for Appointment Making

Set aside time to plan to make phone calls to secure appointments.

Maintain and continually refresh a list of these planned phone calls, together with their objectives and work through this list.

Determine the prior evening which telephone calls you plan to make during the following day, so that you can get started immediately the next day.

Find out when is a good time to reach people, and call them at that time. Be prepared for this to be very early morning, late evening or even weekends. Your tenacity will be rewarded!

If working from home to do this task, get dressed into clothes you would normally wear to make these visits, as it will put you in the 'business mode' when speaking.

Stand up while you make the calls, as a result you will feel, and become, more assertive and effective.

Always secure your next meeting with a customer when you are with them, most likely at the end of the visit after you have offered them a solution they are interested in.

Ask for referrals at this time too. Either co-workers of your existing customers or others in their respective regions, markets, or sectors, they know. A proven method of asking this is:

> *"Who, besides yourself, would you suggest could be interested in solutions such as this?"*

Following their providing you with a referral, we suggest you say something such as:

> *"When I reach out I reach out to them would you mind me saying you'd suggest I contact them?"*

You then have their permission to use their name. They may even offer to contact the referral in advance of you calling them, but try not to lose control of the timing of any call you plan to make. It can be very frustrating to repeatedly ask an existing contact if they've made the call to their suggested new contact and for them to answer that they have either forgotten or not found the time to do this.

Provide existing customers with some rationale of why they would be interested to see you again, for example a new product or service you think would add value to them.

Leave your customers wanting more!

Hints and Tips for Cold Calls

Set aside time to make cold-calls, when the likelihood of rejection is high, limit this to two hours and mentally prepare yourself for this 'rejection period'.

Plan what you'll say during cold-calls and what you'll leave behind for the attention of the contact detail of someone who might be interested, at some future time, in a meeting.

When making cold-calls, develop a script to get past 'gatekeepers' such as security guards, receptionists or secretaries. Some ideas that are proven to work are shown below.

Start by being friendly and say:

"Hello, I wonder if you can help me?"

Smile, pause and then say:

"Who here has responsibility for purchasing/managing/maintaining/ operating/specifying your (insert the relevant words for the situation)...?"

"Are they available to speak with?"

"When would they be available?"

"What is the best way to reach them?"

"What is the best time to make contact with them?"

"What other businesses around here do you know that might be interested?"

Depending on the response to each of the questions you ask, noting that most are open versus closed, you will need to vary your own response and further actions.

Use your mannerisms, smile, appearance, and body language to maximum effect. Amend or adjust these depending on the person you are speaking with, their responses and demeanour.

If you can, try to have fun with this. Recognise that you may need to make multiple such cold-calls to get a contact, appointment or meeting. The reality is that with each rejection you get closer to an acceptance. The more you practise this the better you will become, and the improved results will follow.

A successful salesperson is continually looking to build their contact base through referrals and should always remain alert to opportunities to share their details. They have readily available a brief self, company and product overview, or 'elevator pitch,' that includes the ways in which they have been able to contribute value to their customers.

Summary

Establishing, developing and maintaining an active contact base is fundamental to building a successful sales career. Methods will vary over time, need to take into consideration developments in communications methods, and you will have to ensure you keep pace with these.

You should consider this a crucial activity and set aside the necessary time to plan, prepare, conduct and become comfortable with the various activities we have identified in this chapter. Doing this will positively impact your performance, happiness, career duration and wealth.

CHAPTER SIX

Preparing for Customer Meetings

As explained in the previous section of this book, a significant amount of effort is often required to secure a customer meeting, but for now let us assume that whatever the circumstances regarding how you have been able to organise the meeting, what you're focussing on now is preparing for it.

We have a couple of exercises for you to work on regarding this and, as will be the case throughout this book, we will offer detailed suggestions of ideas or potential solutions, in the pages following each exercise. Therefore, you will be able to combine your own thoughts with these suggestions to develop a 'library' of options in multiple scenarios related to your sales role.

Exercise One — Customer Research Preparation

For this exercise we are assuming that an appointment with a specific customer contact has been secured and that either **you** have never met them previously or it has been over a year since **any** meeting with someone from your company has taken place. The preparation should consider whether the individual has engaged with your organisation previously but not necessarily you directly.

List as many relevant sources of information that you could access prior to visiting a customer to help you better understand their situation and any prior interaction between your companies:

a. **Outside your company records**

b. **Within your company records**

Listed below, in addition to any ideas you may have noted, are some further relevant sources of information that you could consider accessing prior to visiting a customer to help you better understand their situation and any prior interaction between your companies.

a. Outside your company records

Customer's Company website

- Markets served

- Products produced or provided

- Vision, Mission, Values statements

- Corporate responsibilities – environment, people, wider society

- Personnel – possibly the contact name or their ultimate/likely head of function/department

- Industry bodies that they are members of

- Industry standards they hold

- Investment or growth plans – via a blog or 'news' channel

Online Search (Google or another search engine)

Mentions in local and/or national/international press

Contributions to relevant market sector/trade journals

Attendance at trade shows/conferences

White papers produced

Company reports – via formal registration or taxation authorities – your Finance Department can help

'Google' your contact's name to see what information you may uncover about them

Social Media

- Company likely will have a presence on LinkedIn, Facebook, and Twitter – review these for current activities

- Review contact's LinkedIn profile – suggest view in 'private' mode to avoid them knowing you are looking as they may interpret this as intrusive

Typical product portfolio known to be used or likely to be used based on the activities undertaken at the site

Competitors known or likely to be used

b. Within your company records

Prior purchases

Open enquiries

Prior enquiries

Prior quotes or proposals that have been submitted

Colleagues who may have interacted with Company or Contact

Has your Contact or one of their colleagues attended any of your company's Webinars or other on-line event? If so, what topic & when?

Your company's:

Application Library, where available, or knowledgeable colleague to identify any potential specialities or peculiarities you may encounter

Service History records to understand, if any, service support may have been requested or provided previously

CRM records to familiarise yourself with contacts and any other relevant customer information.

CHAPTER SEVEN

Sales Tools or Materials

Having the optimum sales tools with you will help you best explain what your product or service is, how it does whatever it does, why it will benefit the customer and how this may differ from other options they have either used previously, or are considering for future use.

It is therefore surprising to us that, on many occasions, we have observed salespeople who have chosen not to think this through before a visit and ensure they have the best tools available. We have also observed salespeople who, through laziness, choose to leave the best tools behind as "they are too heavy to carry" and then try to explain their product or services by words, hand signals or sketches on a wipe board.

One such situation was when a salesperson had successfully convinced a customer, who shared an office with one of his colleagues who was not in attendance at this initial meeting, of the benefits to him of a particular product. The salesperson was visiting on a follow-up meeting with a detailed proposal for the original customer and was, on this occasion, accompanied by his sales manager. Despite being challenged by his sales manager as to why he wasn't taking the sales tools with him into the visit, he was certain these wouldn't be needed as he'd convinced the customer previously. The salesperson was therefore surprised when the customer's colleague was in the office this time and the original customer asked the salesperson to explain again what was so great about the product.

A very embarrassed salesperson then proceeded to imitate a mime artist using various hand-gestures and explanations that were nowhere near as effective compared with what he would have been able to achieve with the available sales tools. These, in this instance, were a brochure with very clear coloured cut-away drawings that highlighted all the relevant features and their prospective benefits, together with a loosely assembled product sample that the customer could have handled each part of.

A salutary lesson in always being prepared for the unexpected, and of having the right sales tool immediately available!

However, let us continue with the preparation for the customer meeting. Having developed an improved understanding of the customer company and the specific contact we are meeting with, so in the next exercise we will turn to the preparation of what you will need to have with you.

Exercise 2 — Customer Sales Materials Preparation

List the materials you could prepare before going into a customer meeting where you have a general idea of the product, service, or solution likely to be discussed.

Listed below, in addition to the materials you identified, are more examples that could be prepared before going into a customer meeting where you have a general idea of the product, service or solution likely to be discussed.

- Sales Tools (prepared product samples, possibly sectioned where relevant)
- Presentations (in printed or digital format)
- Brochures
- White Papers
- Industry Reports
- Testimonials
- References
- Application Stories
- You Tube Videos

Summary

Spending time preparing for your visit with the customer will provide you with an insight to the people, or person, you are meeting with, their respective position in the company and what their requirements are likely to be, as they relate to your products or services. It will also enable you better understand their company situation, their products and services, their competitors and the market forces they are experiencing, or are susceptible to.

All of the above will position you to ask better informed questions that uncover valuable information, and then develop solutions that will meet their business needs.

This, in turn, will increase your likelihood of successfully selling to them.

Time spent on these activities will be of benefit though it is often overlooked by salespeople, we therefore encourage you to make the effort to achieve this greater level of understanding.

CHAPTER EIGHT

Customer Decision-Making Processes

Successful salespeople identify at an early stage of any opportunity what the decision-making process within a customer is, who is involved and their roles within it.

By so doing, they avoid the, what can seem to be, time consuming and frustrating experience of endlessly chasing the necessary approvals for a customer to actually place a purchase order, even after it *appeared* that a successful sale had been achieved.

We are aware of a situation a few years ago, where a major contractor for an electronics facility was being sold to by an equipment supplier's distributor. The facility personnel claimed that the sub-contractor had total freedom to make their selection of relevant equipment. The distributor paid for and accompanied the person they be lieved to be the key decision-maker within the sub-contractor, with whom they had an existing relationship, to fly trans-Atlantic to their manufacturing facility. They toured with, and entertained them, over several days only to find that the 'real' decision-maker was visiting a competitor's facility in another continent. The circa $2m order, which would have represented about 50% of the distributor's annual sales, was lost, and cost the distributor around $30k in expenses alone, let alone the lost opportunity cost!

The establishing of the process and the varying levels of authority customer personnel have within this, is therefore important. Ultimately, who is the decision-maker?

You may ask yourself:

"How and when should I ensure I'm speaking with the decision-maker?"

The simple answer is relatively early in an engagement and as part of a natural conversation flow with the relevant customer contact.

Questions such as:

- **Who will be involved in the decision-making process?**
- **How does that process work?**
- **What are their roles?**
- **What do you feel is important to them?**
- **What is the budget you are considering for this solution?**
- **When do you anticipate receiving approval for this budget?**

All the above could be applicable to this situation and can therefore be used to establish a clear understanding and avoid either convincing the wrong people or failing to convince the correct people, both of which are likely to result in delays later in the buying process.

A term which was previously used in this context was that to describe someone as the "M.A.N.", meaning that one person had the Money, Authority and Need for any given product, service, or solution.

Though this could still be the case, in most situations, particularly for any sizeable purchase, there are groups of people who, either sequentially, or as a collective, make such decisions.

These are often described as the Decision-Making Unit or D.M.U. and can either be an informal group or in some cases extremely formal, even a 'Committee'. There is no need to fear such groups. Understand what areas to focus on, their interests or concerns, so your proposed solution is appropriately reviewed and ultimately approved.

The process explained in this book can be used whether you are selling to a single decision maker requiring only one meeting, through to a lengthy and complex sales process involving many people, multiple stages, locations, and numerous meetings.

Much has been written on how to sell into companies that use such groups. Fundamentally, identifying their existence, who form them, whether this changes over time and how frequently they meet is what matters to you. Securing the support of an influential member of them as your 'internal coach' will help to guide you towards a successful outcome.

Evidently, ensuring you ask appropriate questions will be essential to understanding this and, in subsequent exercises, we will help you to develop this understanding.

CHAPTER NINE

Objectives for a Sales Visit

Establishing some sensible objectives for a customer meeting, frequently described as either a sales call or visit, is important to ensure that you make appropriate progress towards achieving a level of customer success wherein you and your company are the preferred solution provider for as much of the available opportunities or applications that may exist.

For each visit or meeting therefore, we need to establish a realistic or SMART set of objectives.

We propose using the following approach to describe these objectives:

- **Priority One or P1**
- **Priority Two or P2**
- **Fall-Back**

The P1 and P2 should be focused around the primary reason for the specific visit, with the Fall-Back objective being there in case the meeting is either cancelled, side-tracked or even gate-crashed by either the contacts colleagues or even other salespeople from either competitors or complimentary suppliers – this happens.

These objectives could even be shared with your customer contact as you begin your meeting to establish full transparency and potentially greatly assist you in achieving these.

For example:

P1:	Clarify my understanding of the potential (relevant identified) expansion to include timescales, decision making process, budget, key expectations, personnel involved, and suppliers being considered
P2:	Secure a follow up appointment with key decision makers and influencers to present relevant ideas for the expansion project
Fall-Back:	Identify and understand customer's thoughts and initiatives regarding relevant trend, for example Industry 4.0 (The Internet of Things)

All the above could reasonably be shared with your customer and may help you better understand them and establish your credibility as being someone with a sense of purpose and therefore enhance your potential to add value to the contact and their company/department.

Finally, in addition to the above, being aware of a topical point of interest likely to be relevant to your customer/contact and using this as an 'ice-breaker' either when walking to a meeting place from their reception area or during initial discussions will avoid potentially unnecessary or 'trite' openings such as:

"nice weather today..."

or

"I see the (insert relevant local sports team) finally won..."

Consider how much more professional, especially to a person of seniority with whom you may be meeting for the first time, opening remarks from you such as:

"I see from your website that you're making a significant investment in..., how's that going to affect you?"

or

"what are your thoughts about the latest GDP/PMI (or other relevant industry or financial) data and how does this reflect your business situation?"

So far we have been considering what we can do in preparation for the customer meeting, sales call, or visit. Now let us turn to what will likely happen once we are with the customer. Laid out below is a typical sequence for these meetings, with the phases identified in the 'chevrons' and in the adjacent boxes the activities, or actions, that are likely to take place in each of these to support the structured sales process. This may vary from that shown below, but as a general guide they are a great starting point for us to use.

CHAPTER TEN

Phases of Customer Meetings

Customer Meeting Phases

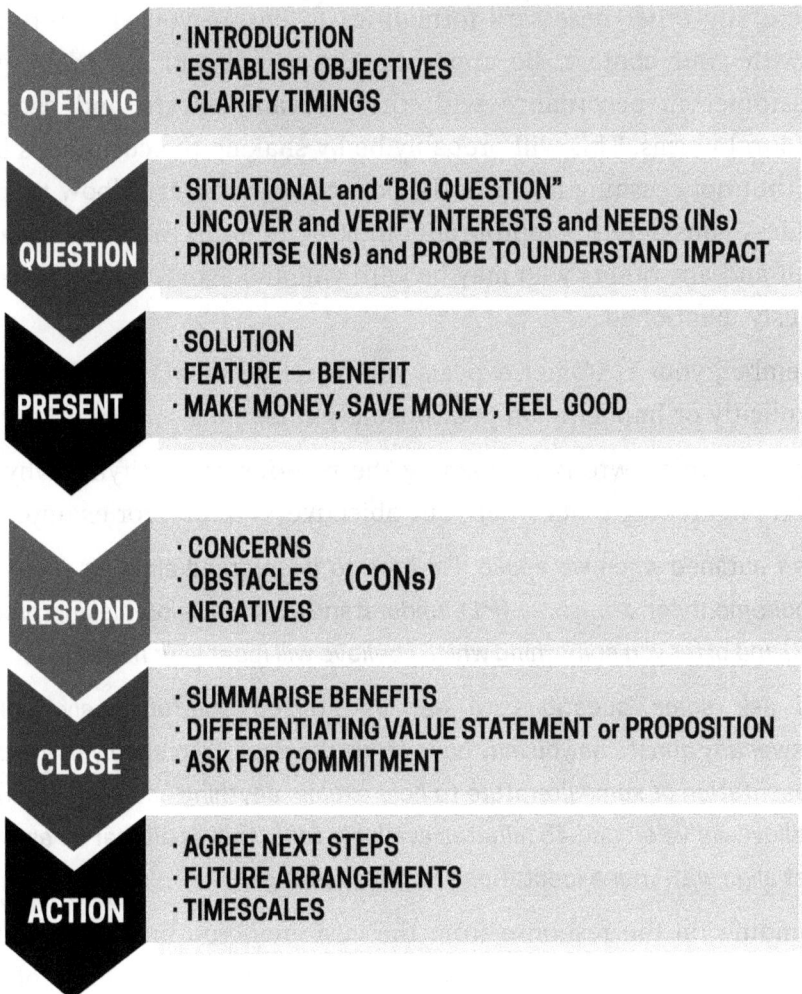

OPENING
- INTRODUCTION
- ESTABLISH OBJECTIVES
- CLARIFY TIMINGS

QUESTION
- SITUATIONAL and "BIG QUESTION"
- UNCOVER and VERIFY INTERESTS and NEEDS (INs)
- PRIORITSE (INs) and PROBE TO UNDERSTAND IMPACT

PRESENT
- SOLUTION
- FEATURE — BENEFIT
- MAKE MONEY, SAVE MONEY, FEEL GOOD

RESPOND
- CONCERNS
- OBSTACLES   (CONs)
- NEGATIVES

CLOSE
- SUMMARISE BENEFITS
- DIFFERENTIATING VALUE STATEMENT or PROPOSITION
- ASK FOR COMMITMENT

ACTION
- AGREE NEXT STEPS
- FUTURE ARRANGEMENTS
- TIMESCALES

Let us explore each of these in more detail.

The Opening

OPENING
· INTRODUCTION
· ESTABLISH OBJECTIVES
· CLARIFY TIMINGS

Arrive on-site early enough to enable you to park, register and complete any other necessary formalities to ensure you are on-time to meet with your contact. Be appropriately attired and equipped, greet the customer in accordance with the relevant culture and accepted behavioural norms. This will probably be by shaking the customer's hand firmly (but not crushing it), or in the post coronavirus era elbow tapping, and unless considered inappropriate, looking them in the eye. Introduce yourself and any others who may be with you and avoid 'trite' remarks as previously mentioned.

Remember, your customer expects you to sell to them, it probably says this explicitly or implicitly on your business card.

There is nothing wrong in opening the meeting by clarifying why you are there, i.e. telling them what your objective(s) is/are, for example:

"As I outlined when we spoke, I'm here to understand all I can about your requirement for a........... (P1), understand your decision-making process (P2) and offer you something which I believe will meet your needs (P1)".

"I'll ask some questions to get us started and obviously look to answer any questions you may have as we progress. I'll probably use either a presentation or some literature to help explain anything I may show you and I believe we've around 45 minutes available to do this. Is all that ok and does that align with your expectations for the meeting?"

Depending on the response from the customer, you may need to wait for others to arrive or they may insist on showing you something of their facility or want to speak about something extremely specific immediately.

As you deem appropriate, you should transition into the next phase of the call, the Questioning element.

Questioning

QUESTION
- SITUATIONAL & "BIG QUESTION"
- UNCOVER & VERIFY INTERESTS and NEEDS (INs)
- PRIORITISE INs and PROBE TO UNDERSTAND IMPACT

Let us take some time to think about questioning in general and why this is so important to any relationship, but in particular to a salesperson's interaction with their customers.

Early in my sales career, I had enjoyed some success selling into a major oil refinery and had managed to arrange a presentation of one of my company's products to the refinery's 'Standards Committee'.

I was delighted to have also managed to have a senior manager, Neil, from the manufacturing company accompany me on this visit and make a presentation to the eight or ten customer personnel I had been advised would attend.

When we had assembled, done all the relevant introductions, were seated and ready to present using a combination of slides, samples and references, my colleague Neil took over. I was expecting him to get into what I describe as an 'angles and dangles', or technical, presentation.

However, he didn't do this. Instead he began by asking a series of questions about what they as a group did, how they went about it, what they looked for when looking at products, how they ensured anything that was new or different, but they felt was of interest, could be used and what were the key things they looked for in this particular type of product.

Initially, I was very uncomfortable, as this wasn't what I'd anticipated or told the meeting organiser we would do. However, after some hesitation, the customer contacts began sharing really useful details that provided us with a deep insight into all their preferences, concerns, experiences and how they contributed to the decision-making process at that site and across their wider organisation.

When Neil subsequently proceeded with the presentation, he was able to relate each specific feature of the product range to the relevant areas of interest, or concern, to the group and this ultimately resulted, some weeks later, in our gaining acceptance of the product on the site and significantly increasing our sales there as a result.

It was one of the most important lessons in sales I have ever learned too. This is to have the courage and confidence to ask the relevant questions, pause to enable the customers to respond, clarify your understanding and only then move to present.

This lesson formed the foundation of what I describe in this book as the 'structured sales process' and undoubtedly helped successfully shape my own sales career.

Let us explore this further.

CHAPTER ELEVEN

Questioning Skills

In his book *"The 7 Habits of Highly Effective People"* author Stephen Covey names one of these as "Begin with the end in mind" and another as "Seek first to understand, then be understood".

Both habits are fundamental to the sales process. Reflect on what the outcomes you are ultimately aiming for because of your involvement. Hopefully, this outcome will be a willing customer engaging with you in order to enable you to provide a solution that meets all their objectives. This in turn will contribute to the long-term success of your company by ensuring you have an increasing customer base that repeatedly uses, and derives value from, your solutions.

However, some customers may be slow or potentially unwilling to share information with you. Therefore, developing your skills as a questioner and active listener are especially important.

In order to fully understand the situation, opportunity, solution requirements, potential concerns and expectations of your customer, it is essential to ask an appropriate number of questions to enable you to offer solution(s) that make it as easy as possible for them to select whatever your proposed solution will be.

In this section we will explore approaches to:

- **Questioning**

- **Listening**

- **Responding**

Types of Questions: Open vs Closed

Open Questions

As you will no doubt be aware, open questions typically begin with the words:

Who

What

Why

Where

When

How

Which

When to use

Asking questions that begin with these words is generally aimed at obtaining multiple pieces of information from your customer that will support the sales process and we describe these as open-ended or "Open" questions.

Therefore, starting an information gathering process would naturally use these types of questions and there are many examples of these we can use that we will develop, and explain, contained in this book.

Closed Questions

These are generally described as questions that are asked to either narrow down a selection or determine a specific response such as 'one' or 'two' or 'yes' or 'no'. These questions can also begin with words that also start an 'Open' question e.g. 'Which of these do you prefer?' so remember that even if you start with one of these 'Open' words, you may end up asking a 'Closed' question.

Objective of the questioning process in a sales scenario

This is to help you to uncover information that will ultimately enable you to offer a relevant solution and explain to your customers how you will help them achieve one or more of the following:

- **Make Money**
- **Save Money**
- **Feel Good**

Therefore, your questions need to start with a broad enough approach that gradually narrows down to the specific requirements of the relevant scenario or opportunity.

We call this a question 'funnelling' process and this can be represented as follows:

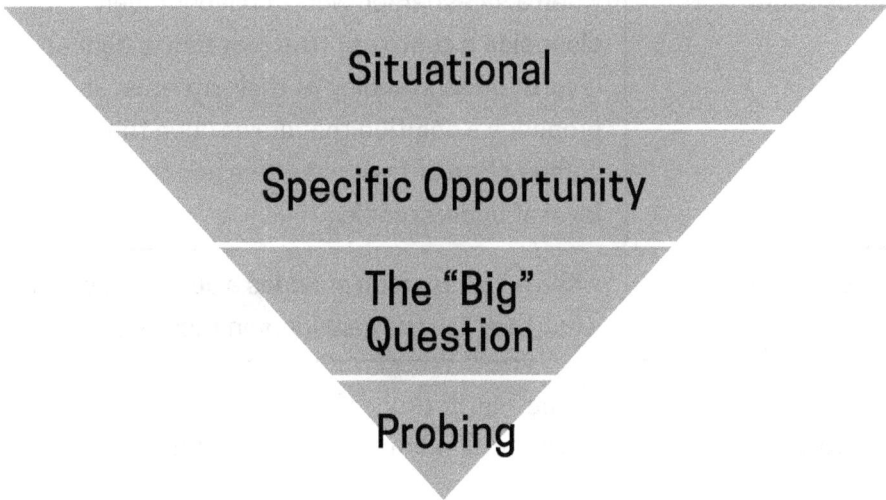

Situational

Specific Opportunity

The "Big" Question

Probing

Insight interviews or Fact-Finds

These are expressions occasionally used to refer to variations of the questioning process. In either case they are extensions of the same basic approach where you're either trying to gain a new insight into the customer's situation, or help them to do so, while ensuring that you gather sufficient information to enable you to develop a fully scoped, relevant, proposed solution that addresses their requirements.

Commonly used types of sales techniques and a brief description of them include;

Insight	when the salesperson helps a customer gain a new insight into how they could achieve success
Solution	when a salesperson provides a solution to their stated needs
Challenger	when a salesperson proposes a very new or fundamentally different method that would otherwise not have been considered by the customer
Consultant	when a salesperson works collaboratively alongside a customer to achieve an enhanced level of understanding of their situation and proposes a solution that draws upon the combination of their expertise and this new level of understanding
Needs Fulfilment	when a salesperson provides a customer with what they tell the salesperson they need

All the above require the gathering of relevant information and therefore it is important to think about the basic funnel above, and apply it in all cases.

In the next two exercises we'll ask you to think about specific questions, that are particularly relevant to your customer, product or service, market, sector or location and, as previously, subsequently give you some ideas that have been used successfully by many sales people in a wide variety of situations.

Initially in Exercise 3, we will explore the general types of questions you could consider when beginning your discussions and then in Exercise 4 we shall dive a little deeper into any specific opportunity that you identify as a result of the initial questions.

Exercise 3 - Situational Questioning

Taking 10 minutes for each, list the questions you could ask that address the following situations as relate to your customer(s):

---

a. **Current Business Situation**

b. **Current Challenges**

c. **Current Opportunities**

---

d. **Future Challenges and Opportunities**

e. **Operational Impact**

f. **Current Supplier/Provider/Technology**

g. **Decision Making Process**

In addition to those you listed, see below examples of questions you could ask that address the following situations:

a. Current Business Situation

How many staff do you have?

What was your turnover or sales last year?

What is your plan for this year?

How does that compare to last year?

What profit would you expect (gross/net)?

Who are your competitors?

Who are your market peers?

Which of the competitors is the strongest? Why?

What other locations or subsidiaries do you have?

What is your typical customer profile?

What is your future business strategy?

Where do you see your business growing in the short/medium term?

Why are you taking this direction?

How long have you been in business?

When does your financial year begin?

What are your key plans for year....?

Where do you see your company in the future?

What share of the (relevant) market do you have?

How is your parent company?

How do you measure success?

What do you see as your strengths?

b. Current Challenges

What are the biggest challenges you face?

What would make a difference in your world?

What are the three most important issues you face today?

What keeps you awake at night?

c. Current Opportunities

What is the capacity of your current operations?

What would you like it to be?

What are your current performance metrics?

How are these tracking currently?

Which of these is the most critical and why?

What would 1% reduction in waste mean to your business (or another relevant industry-wide target)?

What is the cost per Kg of product (or other relevant key financial metric in use that will vary across industries, markets, and sectors)?

d. Future Challenges & Opportunities

What targets have you set the business or department over the coming three years?

What targets have you, your business or department been set over the coming three years?

How will you approach these?

What support do you anticipate needing to achieve these?

When you see something that is new or different, how do you set about being able to use this here?

What do you anticipate will be changing here over the next few months or years?

Where as a business do you feel you are vulnerable?

Where & what are your threats?

Who would be your greatest threat?

e. Operational Impact

What is the capacity or limitations of your current operations?

What would you like it to be?

What are your current performance metrics?

What would 1% increase in plant uptime mean to your business (or another relevant metric)?

f. Current Supplier/Provider/Technology

What are your expectations of key suppliers?

Who is your incumbent partner?

What do they do really well?

What could they improve upon?

g. Decision Making Process

What are the key steps in your decision-making process?

Who gets involved in your decision-making process?

Who makes the final decision?

Who influences the final decision?

Who can veto the decision?

Who approves the decision?

What are the criteria for positive 'yes' decision?

How is any decision reached/made?

What information do you need?

Over what timeframe, typically, are decisions of this type made?

It is   important to take sufficient time to explore several of these questions to ensure you have gained a good understanding of how your customer does whatever it is they are doing currently, how they assess its performance, how they would evaluate any changes they could consider and what impact this could have.

This exercise is structured in a way to encourage you to think about how you would probably do this now and, with the benefit of a number of examples of questions other successful sales people have used, give you some ideas as to how you might go about doing this differently in the future.

We are not advising you to ask all these questions, that would turn it quickly into an interrogation and likely end your ability to work collaboratively with your customer. Instead, select a few that seem to make sense to you and work with these. We have left space so that you can add your thoughts directly into the book if you would like to or of course make your notes separately.

Having identified a specific opportunity for a solution you could possibly provide with your range of products and services, we will move onto some of the more probing questions that are relevant to this particular situation.

Exercise 4 - Specific Opportunity Questioning

Under the various sub-headings, provided for ease of thinking, list the questions you could ask to help you better understand and define this:

a. **General questions about this opportunity**

b. **Questions related to their current practices or how they get the job done today**

Listed below, in addition to those you developed, are some further questions you could ask to help you better understand and define the opportunity:

a. General

What is the job that the investment needs to achieve?

What are your investment return requirements for this?

What do you envisage being your current requirements for the project?

What equipment/processes/activities, if any, will you be replacing?

What are your key priorities as part of the investment?

What is the timeframe you are working with?

What specific issues is this investment or project intended to address?

What effect will solving these issues have on your business?

How will this affect your current practices?

How will rectifying these issues improve your business?

How will you know if this has been successful?

How will you measure success on this project?

b. Current Situation

How do you produce xxxx today?

What equipment/processes/activities are you currently using?

Which type of xxxx are you using?

What is your current output?

What is your current uptime?

How much energy are you currently using?

How do you clean/maintain/operate your existing operations?

What is your current preferred technology?

Who is your current preferred supplier?

How do you measure performance currently?

How do you measure success currently?

Again, as with the prior exercise, you will not need to use all of these questions. Be selective, do not repeat but do ensure you have gathered enough information to understand how your customer measures, understands and describes success. These will be the terms you will need to use when you are seeking to persuade them to select your solution.

CHAPTER TWELVE

The Big Question

What is it and why do we describe it in this way? When you consider that you have sufficient background information using the types of questions we've reviewed so far, it will be necessary to understand, subsequently prioritise and quantify what is important, in the customer's opinion, in order for them to decide whether they will move forward with a particular solution and why they might choose this.

Not asking this question can lead to confusion, inaccurate assumptions, multiple later objections, and lost opportunities – therefore we emphasise the importance of this.

This is a key stage in the customer meeting process and the Big Question needs to be asked, in words which you are comfortable with, and relevant to the customer contact/role/status. Once asked, there is one particularly important thing you should do:

BE QUIET AND LISTEN ATTENTIVELY!

The BIG Question:

"Mr Customer, when you design/specify/select/install/upgrade/ maintain/replace your........., what are the things/factors you take into consideration to help you choose which option/supplier you will use?"

BE QUIET AND LISTEN ATTENTIVELY!

Amend the precise wording of this question to suit your customer and their situation together with your products or services. This could also be described as the 'Killer Question' as if asked it can help you positively progress, if not it could kill the opportunity.

Potential responses to the Big Question

There will be times when the question does not necessarily generate the response you had expected. In these circumstances, do not worry, this is perfectly normal and some of the responses may be as follows:

They will start to tell you what is important to them – their Interests and Needs (INs)

or

"I don't know, I've never really thought about it"

or

"You tell me, you're the expert"

or

"Price – that's the only thing that matters!"

or something else of course.

Regardless, *never* default to providing them with a list of potential Interests and Needs and asking them if these are important to them. Their INs **must** be *their* **INs**, not those that you think they should have. Without their ownership of these they will not stand behind them and agree that having them met will bring about a positive impact for them personally, their project, this opportunity, their department or business.

Below are a series of suggestions to help you maintain momentum in the event it has been stalled by their initial response:

Customer: *"I don't know, I've never really thought about it"*

You: *"That's ok, take a minute to consider and as a reminder I'm looking to get an understanding of what's important to you when you make decisions like this."*

or

Customer: *"You tell me, you're the expert"*

You: *"Well, it's certainly true we work with many customers in your sector, but I'd really like to get an understanding of what's important to you when you make decisions like this"*

If they still choose not to respond, then try:

You: *"We worked with a customer in a similar situation to you recently, what they felt was important to them was...*

(give them one or two examples of INs only) ..." then regroup by asking:

You: *"As those seem relevant to you (gauging their body language or verbal response), what else do you think would be important for you?"*

or

Customer: *Price – that's the only thing that matters.*

You: *"Of course it's important to you, and all our customers, that they spend their company's money wisely. Besides this what else is important to you?"*

So, we have asked the situational questions, identified a potential opportunity that our products and services may be able to satisfy and asked the 'Big Question'. We have been patient and have got the customer beginning to tell us about what is important to them.

We describe these as their Interests and Needs or you may hear them called their Wants & Desires, it's somewhat irrelevant what we call them but very important that we understand these as satisfying them is vital as we'll see.

CHAPTER THIRTEEN

Interests and Needs (INs)

T hese are the things, or factors, that are important to customers and help them determine what option of supplier, technology, or solution to select.

There can be many of these but in general they can all be categorised or listed, under the following four headings, we call **The Big Four:**

1. **Product or Service Characteristics**
2. **Logistical Requirements**
3. **Commercial Expectations**
4. **Personalised Services**

We define these as follows:

1. Product or Service Characteristics

Something specific that the product or service must do for them. These could include be 'easy to operate' or 'easy to maintain', or 'easy to clean', or be 'flexible' to allow varying production rates. There will likely be many of these.

2. Logistical Requirements

These will include the lead time they expect the product or service to be delivered in or provided over. It could include a phased delivery programme or creating a staging point for deliveries. Similarly, it could include the detailed commissioning time needed or a product launch deadline that must be met.

3. Commercial Expectations

This will certainly include the price to be paid, but could also include other elements such as currency, payment timescales, payment phases including the amount of deposit or retention they may prefer. There could also be several specific contractual aspects such as ownership of intellectual property (IP) or warranties that could be grouped here.

4. Personalised Services

Generally, these will include some variation that is totally bespoke to this customer and more typically something that can only be provided or structured by, or through the involvement of, a human being. Examples include provision of a dedicated on-site engineer during commissioning, provision of a dedicated on-call engineer during the first three-months of operations, a design engineer dedicated to them during the design phase of the project.

It helps you to group their Interests and Needs under these four headings as it is likely that you will need a variety of them in order to fully understand what's important, why and what the impact of these being met, or satisfied, is.

Exercise 5 - Examples of Interests and Needs relevant to your products and services

Using the headings below, list as many examples of these potential **Interests** and **Needs (INs)** as you can think of:

a. **Product & Service related**
b. **Logistic related**
c. **Commercial related**
d. **Personalised Service related**

In addition to the examples you may have developed, listed below are examples of potential Interests and Needs (INs). These have been generated from a review of multiple equipment and service providers across multiple industries, selling into many markets, sectors and geographies.

This list is definitely not exhaustive, you will doubtless come across additional examples in your selling activities, but they do give you a starting point. We recommend you develop your own list and engage your colleagues to expand this further, but these will still be useful for you:

a. Product & Service related

Wide range of products

Accuracy

Reliability

High Speed

Flexibility - handle variations of products, speeds, densities, stickiness, densities, sizes

Ease of installation

Ease of maintenance

Clean operation

Cleanability

Compact – space saving

Complete solution provision

Customer product integrity maintained

Integrate another manufacturer's equipment

Performs in noisy, high vibration environment

Environmentally friendly - sustainable

Low power consumption

Low noise generation or quiet operating

Remote monitoring, control and operation

Data security

Readily available remote, on-line, or on-site support and service

Training provided

Readily available spares

Good market reputation

Visually attractive

Project Management provision

b. Logistics related

Manage the installation process

Vary delivery schedules

On time delivery

Split deliveries to multiple locations

Product or project staging (storage of items on or close to site prior to use, enabling immediate availability)

Managed transition of service provision from current provider to new provider

c. Commercial related

Price

Affordable - range of price options

Currency management

Extended or flexible payment terms

Free delivery

d. Personalised Services related

Application experience / expertise

Bespoke solutions developed

Regulatory guidance

On-site support in relevant phase

Product trials

Product flow analysis

Project design

Dedicated service engineer after installation

On-site resident engineering support

Dedicated contact via help line

Regular performance reports

It is very common to miss something a customer shares with us.

Why is this and what can we do to improve our ability to absorb information being shared with us?

This happens when we're thinking about what we're trying to accomplish, or maybe a sales process we are getting used to or even trying for the first time. It could be we are pre-occupied thinking of the presentation we know is coming. Even distracted by what we consider the customer, or an accompanying colleague or boss, is thinking of us.

What we miss could be something really important related to what our customers are thinking, their experience of us, or our competitor, a problem they reference but don't initially identify or explain, their decision making process and budget. Or anything else that could be relevant and potentially provide for you the awareness of a key motivator for them to use your product or service solution.

We have discussed questioning and highlighted the importance of this, but evidently our ability to really listen to what the customer says, not only in response to our questions, but what they may share with you at any time, is potentially even more important.

CHAPTER FOURTEEN

Listening Skills

There is a risk that because we're so focussed on asking the right questions at the right stage in the sales process, that we may let our attention wander away from what the customer says and therefore miss something extremely important to us.

Therefore, we should practice what are described as '**active listening skills**'.

Active listening is all about building rapport, understanding, and trust. By learning and practising the skills below, you will become a better listener and actually hear what your customer is saying, not just what you think they are saying or what you want to hear.

Steps to Better Active Listening Skills

Below are eleven different skills for effective listening. You do not have to become adept at each of these skills to be an effective listener, but the more you do, the better you will be. If you even use three or four of these skills, you will find yourself listening, hearing and absorbing more of what another person is saying to you and, as it relates to a sales situation, you'll pick up more information about their Interests and Needs. This ability will be of significant value to you later in the sales process when you will be dealing with objections or obstacles.

1. Restating

To show you are listening, repeat every so often what you think the customer said, not by 'parroting' or repeating word for word what they've said, but by paraphrasing what you heard in your own words. For example, "Let's see if I'm clear about this. . ."

2. Summarizing

Bring together the facts and pieces of the situation to check understanding. For example, "So it sounds to me as if..." Or, "Is that it?"

3. Minimal encouragers

Use brief, positive prompts to keep the conversation going and show you are listening. For example, "umm-hmmm," "Oh?" "I understand," "Then?" "And?"

4. Reflecting

Instead of simply repeating, reflect the customer's words in terms of feelings. For example, "This seems really important to you. . ."

5. Giving feedback

Let the person know what your initial thoughts are on the situation. Share pertinent information, observations, insights, and experiences. Then listen carefully to confirm.

6. Emotion labelling

Putting feelings into words will often help a person to see things more objectively. To help the person begin, use "door openers". For example, "I'm sensing that you're feeling concerned...passionate...anxious..."

7. Probing

Ask questions to draw the customer out and get deeper and more meaningful information. For example, "What do you think would happen if you...?"

8. Validation

Acknowledge the customer's problems, issues, and feelings. Listen openly and with empathy, and respond in an interested way. For example, "I appreciate your sharing this with me..."

9. Effective pause

Deliberately pause at key points for emphasis. This will tell the customer that they are saying something that is important to you.

10. Silence

Allow for comfortable silences to slow down the exchange. Give the customer time to think as well as talk. Silence can also be immensely helpful when a customer seems unwilling to share information. We have observed many salespeople being really uncomfortable with silence. They feel obligated to fill this by speaking and by doing so they remove the opportunity to learn. Be patient, have the courage to pause even if this feels uncomfortable initially and let the customer share their thoughts.

11. Consequences

Part of the feedback may involve talking about the possible consequences of inaction. Take your cues from what the customer is saying. For example, "What happened the last time you stopped regularly maintaining the xxxx?" or "If you chose to do nothing about this, what would be the situation in two to three months?"

Having asked a series of questions including the 'Big Question', actively listened throughout and taken notes as appropriate, we will have uncovered a number of their Interests and Needs and categorised these under the headings of the 'Big Four', so can we now proceed to share a potential solution with them by presenting our product or service?

This may seem like the right time to do this but let us consider a couple of things.

Firstly, have you been able to uncover INs under each of the categories of the 'Big Four'?

If not, then you may struggle to later justify how your product and service will add value and make a positive impact to the customer. Remember virtually all of us have competitors, or even if we're the first in the market with our product, the customer is probably doing what they do now in a way that does not involve our products, and therefore will still require persuading to make a change.

We advise salespeople to ensure they have at least three **IN**s under each of the '**Big Four**' categories before they proceed past this point, though this will vary depending on your products and services, how well the customer is known to you and their particular situation.

Secondly, we must understand which of the **IN**s are most important to them and crucially, why this is so?

Finally, we need to understand and quantify, what either positive or negative, impact will arise for the customer if these are satisfied or not.

Only after all three of the above are achieved should you move to present a solution.

Let us explore this a little further.

CHAPTER FIFTEEN

Verifying Interests and Needs (INs)

It is highly probable that you could anticipate what the customer will tell you is important to them; you could even tell them in advance what they will likely say. However, what is fundamental at this stage is that the customer needs to 'own' these and tell you in their own words what they're thinking in response to either the **Big Question** or other questions you pose.

By having the customer 'own' these, you can then use these later in the sales process, as you present your solution, to link a specific feature to a benefit which they have told you is important to them, since the benefit will address the Interests and Needs they previously said were significant.

If you try to link features to benefits that address **INs** they have *not* said are important, there's a high probability they will discount these, either openly or potentially more damagingly silently, as you won't realise this, and you will begin to lose control of the sales process without necessarily noticing or understanding why.

It is, therefore, particularly important to allow time for the customer to respond and reaffirm what they are telling you by using one of the techniques we discussed under 'active listening'. Typically, by summarising, paraphrasing, and getting acknowledgement from the customer what their **INs** are, you can **verify** what is truly of interest to them.

Statements, such as:

"If I'm understanding you correctly what's important to you is that you're looking for a Flexible solution, that enables you to vary production capacity while maintaining Operational Efficiency over a sustained period in a Reliable manner?"

If the customer agrees with you then you will have verified these **INs** and got agreement that these are important.

So, should you stop there and move to presenting a potential solution?

No, not yet.

Keep probing to establish all their potential INs.

Simple follow-up questions or statements, such as:

What else?

Anything more?

Keep going...

will likely have the customer tell you more and enable you to identify further **INs**.

As a general guide, it will be important to generate between three and six **INs** which could be categorised as being related to the Product or Service, and at least one, though ideally two or three, under the other three headings of Logistics, Commercial and Personalised Service.

Once you feel you have **uncovered** and **verified** an appropriate number of **INs** and these are sufficiently varied to enable you to proceed, then we need to do two more things:

1. Understand the **priorities** of their **INs**

2. Understand the **impact** of these being satisfied or not – sometimes we describe this as their 'pain'.

CHAPTER SIXTEEN

Prioritising Interests and Needs

By understanding what is of most importance, and therefore potential impact, it will enable you to focus on the relevant Features and Benefits of your products and services that will be the most memorable to the customer and be more likely to persuade them that your solution is the one they should choose.

Most people can readily remember three key elements, topics, or pieces of information they will have been exposed to during a conversation or presentation.

Therefore, if we can distil the list of verified INs to establish the top three priorities, then we have a better chance of retaining their attention, and therefore persuading them to select any solution we may present.

Asking an appropriate question, combined with active listening techniques, will enable this. For example:

"Of all these things you've indicated that are important to you, what would you say are the top three?"

Or

"If you had to prioritise these, which would be most important to you?"

Then, summarising these in their order of priority will ensure you are aligned with the customer on these **verified**, and now **prioritised**, INs.

For example:

*"That's interesting. So of these areas of interest, having a **Flexible** product that allows you to vary production capacity, and that we provide regular **Service** to ensure your **Operational Uptime** for you, are of most importance?"*

There is no reason why you should not have more than three areas of priority but be aware that not everything can be a true priority and somewhere compromises will likely need to be made.

We then need to move onto understanding *why* certain things are of priority by probing further to understand, either the positive impact of these being met, or potentially the negative consequences of them not being so.

CHAPTER SEVENTEEN

Understand Customer Impact

There will be an impact to your customer, sometimes described as their pain, of whatever decision they choose to make, including making no decision. The better they understand this, with your support, the more likely it is they will make a decision that will involve a solution you can provide.

The impact of their decision can be quantified in some manner, likely either operationally or financially but sometimes in another less readily identifiable manner.

If you can help them quantify the impact, then when it comes to asking them to make a decision in your favour the more likely they will select your solution and enable you to become a valued supplier, partner, solution provider or friend.

Ideally, as mentioned previously, we are looking to understand the impact, expressed in a **quantifiable financial** or **operational** manner, of these **verified** and **prioritised** INs being met, or not.

This information will enable you to relate these to the customer when, as is highly likely, you need to justify the price you are seeking to charge the customer for your solution.

As we will see later, we will ultimately describe the likely impact in one or more of the following ways. You will be able to help them:

Make Money

and/or

Save Money

and/or

Feel Good

It is always easier to gather this quantifying type of information earlier in the selling process before you have made a presentation of a potential solution, rather than after this, as customers are then less likely to divulge this type of information because they may have begun to find reasons not to select your proposed solution.

Therefore, again using 'active listening' techniques, we can ask questions such as:

"You indicate that......(name the relevant IN)... is really important, why is that? What would be the impact of this being provided or not?"

followed by:

"How could you quantify or measure this?"

and:

"What, or who, else would be impacted by this?"

Pay careful attention to their responses and note these down for future reference, as it is likely you will need to expand upon these to support your price justification argument.

We will not dive into great detail on this aspect at this stage, but being able to 'drill down' sufficiently to get a simple value, such as an increase in production capacity, reduced product loss rate, saving in labour-hours or improvement in production efficiency will enable these to be accumulated and presented, to support your sales proposal.

Exercise 6 - Probing to Fully Understand Impact

a. **List several questions you could use to probe at this stage in the sales process:**

b. **List the types of information you would be seeking to draw from your customer in response to these questions:**

Examples in addition to those you developed:

a. **Several questions you could use to probe at this stage in the sales process:**

What would an increase in production rates mean to your site?

Who else would be impacted if this were achieved?

If you were able to reduce the shut-down time by…what would that mean to the capacity?

How many labour-hours are currently spent doing a product changeover?

What is the fully loaded labour rate for this site?

What rate of OEE (Operation and Equipment Efficiency) are you currently achieving?

What is the target rate of OEE for this site/line?

What is the rate of product give-away or wastage currently?

What is the target rate?

How is the effectiveness of your department/site/team/product measured?

How do feel about this and what are the target rates?

How do you measure productivity or efficiency or utilisation currently?

What is the typical internal rate of return you look to achieve when making investments, what is the timeframe for these and how do you measure this?

b. **Types of information you would be seeking to draw from your customer in response to these questions:**

Product loss or wastage rates

Product loss or wastage values

Labour -hour rates used on site/line/department

OEE values

Variations of target data desired

Value of product sales per line/pack/hour/week/person

Value per Kg of product

Productivity, efficiency, or utilisation rates

Methods of calculating the above rates

Investment return rates methods of measurement and times

So, we are at the stage where we have done the following:

As a result of asking situational, the 'Big Question' and various further probing questions we've uncovered, verified, prioritised and quantified the impact of a number of Interests and Needs and are confident that they are sufficiently varied to cover the 'Big Four' of these adequately.

Now, we are ready to present a solution to our customer, so let us consider a few fundamentals first.

CHAPTER EIGHTEEN

Presenting Solutions

PRESENT
- · SOLUTION
- · FEATURE — BENEFIT
- · MAKE MONEY, SAVE MONEY FEEL GOOD

There are three basic principles to presenting that are relevant to any type of presentation:

1. **Tell them what you are going to do**

2. **Do it**

3. **Tell them what you have done**

Applying this simple approach ensures aligned expectations and, in a sales scenario, enables a smooth and appropriately timed transition to a presentation.

When to transition to the solution presentation

Once you have uncovered and verified an appropriate number and range of INs.

Remember, as a guide, this should be between four and six related to the specific Product or Service being discussed, plus at least one each, ideally more, related to Logistics, Commercial and Personalised Service

How to transition

Make a statement, or ask in the form of a question:

"Let me show you something which, based on our discussions and what you've indicated is important to you will, I believe, be particularly relevant to you/your situation."

Tools to use

From the sales tools you may have available, select the most appropriate and explain that you will use this, or these, to help you explain to them the proposed solution. Say how long it will likely take and encourage them to ask any questions they may have, either as you go along, or once you've completed this. Use your own judgement of the situation, the individual or group you are with, as it relates to handling questions. Though generally, it is our experience that addressing questions as they arise, in a sales scenario, is preferred as this prevents potential concerns from 'derailing' your presentation.

It may be that you have a colleague with you who has some subject matter expertise, e.g. Product Manager, Senior Sales Person/Manager or Key Account Manager who will make the presentation so again introduce them and what they will do at this stage accordingly.

Basic Process

If you are selling a product, then a high-level overview of what the product is, what it does, how it achieves this and of course how this meets the verified, prioritised and quantified needs that the customer has is your objective.

If you have a service, or intangible product, then this will be a very similar approach, with a high level overview of what this is, how the service is provided, by whom, over what period of time, how it achieves this and of course how this meets the verified, prioritised and quantified needs that the customer has is again your objective.

Let us get into more detail because the key difference between how to present for explanation, such as in a training course or at a college, and how to present for selling, is that ultimately you are seeking to persuade your 'audience' that your product or service will add sufficient value to them or their business, to enable them to confidently spend their money with you. Remember, they always have a choice whether they do this, and further, when they choose to do this.

There is a structure we propose that can be used to good effect regardles s of the product or service you are selling. This uses a tried and tested approach that, though certainly not unique is, if done well, proven to lead to an improved success rate in securing sales as a result.

We will begin this by reviewing the fundamentals, what are you going to present?

Most businesses provide several different materials that can or could be used to present their products or services. We call these 'Sales Tools' and we'll develop this concept a little further now.

In the next exercise, we're asking you to list all the examples of potential sales tools that you can think of that are available to you, then we'll explore some further ideas for your consideration, and discuss how to use these to best effect.

Product or Service Knowledge

The more detailed knowledge you have of your product or service, including the variety of ways it can be used in as broad a range of applications, or circumstances, then the more you will be able to pay attention to your customer, their responses to your presentation, and suggestions, their questions and body-language.

Therefore, although we are focussing on the sales process in this book, do not under-estimate the importance of your detailed product or service knowledge, they are both important. Further, having strength in product knowledge will free your mind up to enable you to develop the confidence in your sales skills, and quickly resolve misunderstandings, or concerns, that a customer may have.

Exercise 7 - Sales Presentation Tools or Materials

List the sales tools you have, or could have, available to assist you to present a solution to a customer either:

a. **At an initial meeting at customer premises or a location where either a demonstration piece of equipment or other tangible evidence, for example an office or factory tour, is not available**

b. **At your company's facilities, for example a customer centre, company offices, warehouse, or factory**

In addition to those you may have identified, listed below are some examples of sales tools you may have, or could have, based on widely available sales tools used to present a solution to a customer either:

a. **At an initial meeting at customer premises or a location where either a demonstration piece of equipment or other tangible evidence, for example an office or factory tour, is not available**

Company overview brochure

Product range overview brochure

Specific product brochure

Brochure targeted at specific applications or markets

Product samples

- Loosely assembled to enable dismantling
- Sectioned or cut-away to enable internal view

Product presentations – PowerPoint or other

Product drawings

Company videos

YouTube videos

Company organisation charts

White papers (detailed technical articles)

Sales Presenters – assembled folders containing printed drawings, slides, or other materials

Company website

Customer testimonials – provided by a customer

Case studies – written about a customer experience

b. **At your company's facilities, for example a customer centre, company offices, warehouse, or factory**

Company overview static presentation

Product samples, similar to above but either larger or greater range

- Loosely assembled to enable dismantling
- Sectioned or cut-away to enable internal view

Application 'mock-ups'

Company tour of offices and any other facilities

Senior management introductions

As can be seen, there are many sales tools that are likely to be available and, while the prior examples are not intended to be exhaustive, we encourage you to keep developing ideas for sales tools as needed. Urge your managers, or marketing teams, to work with you to provide these to support your sales efforts.

However, one of the most common and unfortunate situations we observe is that even though there may be a wide number of these available for a sales person to use, they either don't use them at all or they don't use them effectively.

The reasons for their non, or ineffective, use vary but predominantly these are either (i) laziness - the sales person doesn't want to carry them around, (ii) unfamiliarity - the sales person doesn't know they're available or how best to use them and finally (iii) lack of confidence in the face of a customer.

The first two are reasonably easy to address; make the effort to take these with you and put the effort in to learn these in detail.

The third reason, a lack of confidence when with a customer, typically either comes from unfamiliarity with the sales tools in which case, as previously stated, make the effort to become familiar with these. Or it can sometimes be that the sales person feels there will be a break in the natural 'flow' of the meeting if they take a sales tool from their 'bag' or start their pc/tablet, to make a presentation.

If this is the case, practise making a natural transition into this phase of the meeting, or discussion, as we mentioned earlier by using a 'transition' statement such as:

"Let me show you something which based on our discussions and what you've indicated is important to you will, I believe, be particularly relevant to you/your situation."

Do this as part of the conversation and ensure, if you are going to use devices that they are charged, configured so they will start quickly and that you are familiar with their operation.

Let us assume you are now ready to go, and get into the structure previously mentioned.

CHAPTER NINETEEN

Feature – Benefit

M ost products, services and/or solutions have many specific Features, (reminder: *something that you can see or touch,*) that can provide an even larger number of specific **Benefits**, (reminder: *answers the customer's question "what does this do for me?" or "what's in it for me" (WIIFM)*), for customers in a range of scenarios.

Initially, as previously suggested, provide a brief high level overview of your product or service. Then move to focus your presentation on the features that will meet the specific verified, prioritised and quantified INs. Explain how a specific feature meets the applicable IN, and why this is of benefit to the customer in their specific circumstances.

This does not mean you avoid mentioning something that may be pertinent, but your focus should be on those aspects which they have confirmed are most important to them.

Take your time, ensure your customer is following you, observe their body language to gauge their acceptance and regularly pause to ensure you are being understood.

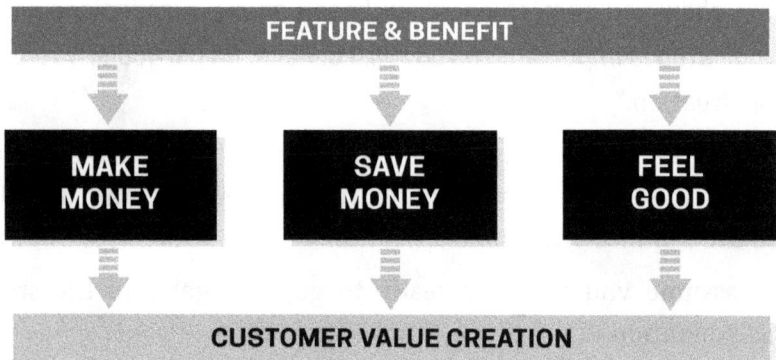

FEATURE & BENEFIT

| MAKE MONEY | SAVE MONEY | FEEL GOOD |

CUSTOMER VALUE CREATION

CHAPTER TWENTY

Make Money, Save Money, Feel Good

When we introduced the importance of probing to understand the impact of an Interest or Need being met, we discussed how important it is to explain how your solution will achieve one or more, or possibly all of the above. This thereby explains how this will create value for the customer, as defined by them.

Your presentation is where you will bring these statements together in the form of connections or links.

We maintain this approach as represented by the prior images and those below for each of the relevant features, until we are confident that we have met their prioritised Interests and Needs and that the links, via the benefits to the creation of value via the Make Money, Save Money and Feel Good are accepted.

FEATURE (MEETS IN)	BENEFIT (WIIFM)	MAKE MONEY SAVE MONEY FEEL GOOD

If you can make these links in a comfortable, conversational manner, the impact of your sales presentation will increase dramatically. You will effectively combine appropriate features with the derived benefits of meeting their INs and quantifying the positive impact for their business.

Initially, we advise going through this in the order described above, but there is no reason why you cannot re-order these elements of the explanation, provided they are all there.

For example:

"You can see these specially treated stainless steel hoppers (Feature) that reduce product sticking (Benefit), therefore improve throughput (Make Money), and typically lead to a reduced product loss rate of 15% an hour (Save Money), which could mean as much as a £300 per hour gain for you (Make Money)."

Could become:

"You mentioned reducing product loss rate as being important to you (Save Money). A reduction of 15% per hour (Save Money), equating to a gain of £300 per hour (Make Money) can be achieved as a result of these specially treated stainless-steel hoppers (Feature) reducing product sticking (Benefit)."

Or:

"As a result of our having over 400 service engineers (Feature) in the region all connected via our systems to our operations centre (Feature), therefore improving our responsiveness enabling us to meet your one-hour response time (Benefit), and ensure you achieve your productivity targets (Make Money) could mean as much as a £300 per hour gain for you (Make Money) versus the two hours lost currently."

Could become:

"You mentioned reducing production loss while waiting two hours for a service engineer visit as being important to you (Make and Save Money). A reduction of this wait by one hour, equating to a gain of £300 for this hour (Make Money) can be achieved as a result of the way we organise, coordinate and deploy our service team (Feature and Benefit)."

We describe the above types of statements as '**Differentiating Value Propositions**' and we will cover these, their importance, and how to use them in more detail later.

Feeling Good

What do we mean by this? In this context, it is something that in addition to a quantified value of either making or saving money, can help to persuade the customer in favour of your proposed solution.

Examples of this could be:

- Improving safety
- Taking work away from them personally or from their staff
- Creating a favourable impression of them amongst their colleagues or superiors
- Freeing them up to pursue more 'core' tasks
- Eliminating non-core, or mundane, tasks
- Simplifying their role or life
- Enabling them to sleep better due to removing a persistent concern or worry

FEATURE (MEETS IN) → BENEFIT (WIIFM) → MAKE MONEY SAVE MONEY FEEL GOOD

Maintain an appropriate pace during the presentation, noting the responses of our customer to gauge their level of agreement with each element, before transitioning via the Respond phase, into what we describe as the Close phase of the visit.

Before we discuss this, let us consider four further things that will be relevant at this stage:

1. Buying Signals
2. Unique Selling Points
3. Positive and Negative differentiators
4. Concerns, Obstacles and Negatives (CONs)

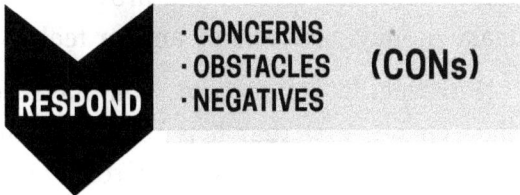

RESPOND

- CONCERNS
- OBSTACLES **(CONs)**
- NEGATIVES

Buying Signals

A buying signal is an indication from a customer that something is of particular interest, or relevance, to them.

They can be in the form of words, for example:

"that's interesting" or "I've never seen that before" or "yes, that's what I'm looking for" or "at last!" or "mmmm..."

Or they could be a gesture, such as:

a nod of the head, a smile or leaning forwards in their chair.

It is important you closely observe your customer and recognize any buying signals, as this will help you to ensure your presentation remains relevant to the customer and their situation.

Unique Selling Points (USPs)

This is an expression commonly used in association with products or solutions in markets with multiple competitors and, therefore invariably, alternative solutions. However, it is increasingly difficult to establish and retain something that is truly unique, as over time similar products or solutions enter the market.

Do not assume that your customer necessarily knows which features of your product are unique, or that they know your competitors products so well that they can readily discount a feature of yours as not being unique.

In other words, avoid selling for your competition, make them work as hard as you do to explain their solution to this particular customer. In all likelihood, they will not.

Therefore, have faith in the structured sales process. When you ask relevant questions, you'll uncover their INs, so you can present a solution that meets their needs, and provide them with relevant benefits. They'll make money, save money and/or feel good.

However, if you believe you have something that is truly unique, then ensure first that it is relevant, otherwise it may be discounted or considered unnecessary or expensive, and then reinforce your presentation with this or these aspects – but don't make claims that you can't substantiate or support with proof of uniqueness.

Positive and Negative Differentiators

These are terms to describe where a specific feature of your product or service solution is superior (positive) or inferior (negative) in comparison with what you know one of your potential competitors can provide.

It is important that we therefore build upon our positive differentiators, to offset what may be negative ones.

However, as with the prior notes related to USPs, don't assume that either the customer knows your competitor's product well enough to recognise what are the Positive or Negative differentiators, or that the competitor salesperson will take the time to explain this.

If therefore, you build your presentation focused around your positive differentiators, you will likely create strong momentum in your favour with the customer, and it is this momentum that is the key to gaining agreement for your product, service and solution to be accepted. Remember, your objective is to tip the balance of your customer's thoughts in your favour, not necessarily prove beyond all doubt, this is not a court of law!

Concerns, Obstacles and Negatives (CONs)

As you progress through your presentation, it is highly likely and indeed desirable that your customer expresses one or more of the above as without doing this it is unlikely that a they will have a serious intent of proceeding to purchase, or specification.

In our experience, it is probably better to pause and address these as they arise. Otherwise, there is a high risk that the customer will 'tune out' of what you are saying until, and unless, they have their issue answered appropriately.

Therefore, a suggested approach is as follows:

1. **Pause, ask the customer to restate or confirm their concern, obstacle or negative (CON)**

2. **Ask them why that is important to them, you may discover something new**

3. Ask them to explain what the potential impact of this is to them. This may potentially be new information for you

4. Replay this back to them, without needlessly agreeing with whatever they've told you, in your own words, to make sure you have fully understood their point or concern

5. If you have an answer that you can provide, or an explanation that you can offer, do so and then ask them if that addresses their concern, obstacle or negative

6. **If it does, summarise where you had got to previously, and proceed**

If it does not, ask again for them to clarify and proceed again as above.

If there is no credible response you can provide at that time, in a situation where your product or service cannot do what they need, then restate the capabilities that you do have and link these to the INs that you'd previously uncovered, verified and prioritised, explaining how these will provide a positive impact as previously established.

Then ask again, whether with that clarification, they are happy to continue discussing this potential solution.

If so, then carry on.

If not, then establish precisely what it is that they need to see, hear, or understand and confirm that without this they could not use your solution as presented. Ensure you pause here to allow for sufficient time for their careful reflection. Is the missing element truly indispensable or could they manage without it? Do they need to check this with their colleagues?

In our experience, many of these apparent obstacles can be eliminated by using the above process since the customer may be expressing what could be considered as "nice to have" versus "must have" requirements.

However, if you currently cannot satisfy this "must have" requirement, offer to withdraw, and return when, or if, you are able to meet that specific requirement. This may be necessary and is a far more professional way to proceed. It ensures you maintain your integrity in such situations as opposed to making 'empty' promises that you will not be able to meet.

We know of a situation where an experienced salesperson said to their customer:

"I believe there is a way for us to do what you need, but right now, I'm just not sure how. Can I go away, ask some colleagues, do some research, find the solution and then return?"

The customer agreed, the salesperson developed the solution with the support of his colleagues, returned as agreed in principle, presented the solution and the customer placed the order.

This was a great example of humility, integrity, resourcefulness, resilience and ultimately success.

This is why sometimes this process can take several weeks, months or even years as you look for further relevant examples of comparable situations that demonstrate the positive impact of this solution, or as your own products or services develop so that they can do so.

However, maintaining control of the situation and obtaining the customer's permission to re-engage will build your integrity and professionalism in their view, and greatly assist you in long-term relationship building in this context, as it did in the example.

Re-engaging after a delay

When in the situation of needing to re-engage with a customer after a delay, which is possible for a variety of reasons, you will not need to go through the entire structured sales process. It will be necessary, and important, to summarise the previous meeting, check that the INs, priorities, impact and accepted benefits remain as before. There may have been some developments in the customer's situation since you last met with them, or there could be new people for you to meet, in which case again summarise with an introduction such as:

"When 'Mr. Customer A' and I met last time, they shared with me that the following were requirements any solution would need to satisfy: (repeat the previously prioritised INs), how do those sound to you?"

Give the new contact(s) time to consider and share their thoughts with you. If there are new INs to be aware of, review these together with the previously accepted ones and gain agreement. If their needs have changed, explore the impact of these being met or not and seek quantification of the impact if these are met or not, as previously.

Or, if there are no new additional contacts:

"When we met last time, you shared with me that the following were requirements any solution would need to satisfy: (repeat the previously prioritised INs), has anything happened that would change these?"

Highlight additional features and benefits to address any new INs they may have shared you, then proceed in the same manner as previously, with an appropriate presentation concluding with your Differentiating Value Proposition or Statement (explained fully in the 'Close section), possibly amended to reflect any new INs that were agreed as being of priority.

If you are re-engaging because you were unable to provide a solution that met the relevant INs during your prior meeting, then the approach of initially summarising where you were previously as a starting point, moving on to explain whatever new information related to your solution and linking via Feature – Benefit – Make Money, Save Money, Feel Good – Differentiating Value Proposition, remains consistent.

Having done this, seek to 'Close' using the relevant statement or question and therefore progress to the 'Action' phase.

The above method will ensure you remind customers of what they had indicated was important to them, allow for any changes in circumstances to be reflected in your presentation and proposal and, very importantly, demonstrates that you have taken notice of what they say without making assumptions that may be incorrect. This will enable you to maintain momentum and solidify your relationship with the customer(s).

CHAPTER TWENTY-ONE

Closing

CLOSE
- SUMMARISE BENEFITS
- DIFFERENTIATING VALUE STATEMENT or PROPOSITION
- ASK FOR COMMITMENT

E ntire books and courses exist on this topic and there are many differing theories and perspectives on what is an effective 'close' and when to use it.

We will simplify this concept here and provide some straightforward examples that you can use as they are, or modify them to suit you, your style, your customer and/or scenario.

A close is a statement or question that you use in order to establish whether or not a customer has heard enough information to persuade them to commit to buying your solution, or to approving it from their perspective. Thereby enabling the sales process to progress to the next stage within a customer's buying process, which may be to place the order, or proceed to a further review stage.

You will need to judge when to use such a statement or question. We provide some examples below, but generally if you're receiving positive buying signals from the customer and you believe that you have sufficient positive momentum gained from addressing their verified and prioritised INs, explaining their Make Money, Save Money or Feel Good Benefits and addressed any of the Concerns, Obstacles or Negatives (CONs) previously referred to, then it is a good time to try.

Close or Trial Close?

A Close becomes a Trial Close when, having made the statement or asking the question, the customer is not yet ready to proceed to commit. So therefore, every Close can become a Trial Close or vice-versa, you will not know until you try.

Closing Statements or Questions:

In all cases, start by summarising the accepted benefits that the customer has agreed with as you made your presentation & then for example say:

"What do we need to do now to move this forward?"

Or

"How can we take this to the next step?"

Or

"In order to meet the timescales, we discussed, we'll need to begin working on this by ...(insert date)... will you go ahead and get the order process started?"

Or

"How can I help you get this started so that we can meet your timeframe?"

Or

"With your support, can I get the ball rolling on this?"

Or

"What else do you need from me in order to get everything started?"

Then wait for the response. Depending on this, you can either retrace your prior steps focusing on any area of concern, before again summarising the accepted benefits and trying again.

Handling Objections

Despite your best efforts, it is possible your customer may not be prepared to move forwards immediately. Based on the market situation, and how you are positioned, one of the most likely concerns, or objections, will be price.

Our objective is to get you so familiar with this situation that you welcome this objection, and indeed 'force' it, as we mentioned in the early overview of the structured sales process. With practise you will see this as a tremendous opportunity to reinforce the value your solution provides the customer.

During the initial presentation, we may not have sufficient information to quote an accurate price. However, you should be able to outline an approximate price, or price range, that the customer can use to make any comparisons against either prices they have previously paid, their budget, or competitive quotes they may be in possession of.

Therefore, be proactive. When you have completed your presentation, if the customer has not asked the 'how much will this cost me?' question but has indicated they're accepting of the remainder of the presentation, then try asking something like:

"Typically, this kind of solution, depending on several factors which we can review, would be in the order of...$/£/€... How does that compare with your budget/expectations/prior experience?"

Assuming that the customer responds by saying that this is more than they had expected, you should restate their verified and prioritised INs and the positive impact on them of these being met, remind them of the specific Features, Benefits and Make Money, Save Money or Feel Good quantifications and use this to justify, not necessarily the total price, but the difference between their expectations and your price range.

As with most scenarios we are not familiar with, this will seem stressful initially but after relatively few attempts it will begin to feel more comfortable and eventually almost second nature to you.

Therefore, a form of words such as:

"Mr Customer, you explained to me that...(list their verified and prioritised INs)... were really important to you. I've shown you how this...(name the product or service)... meets these because of the ...(list the relevant Features) ... and further provides you with the Benefits of...(list these). These will also lead to you being able to...(explain and quantify how they Make Money, Save Money or Feel Good, providing a positive impact for them)... Therefore, can you see how this is actually exceptionally good value and would be a wise decision for you?"

will be effective to remind your customer why your proposed solution should be considered favourably by them. You can then regain the positive momentum and progress to the "Call to Action" phase.

Differentiating Value Propositions or Statements

The above is a good example of such a statement in that it clearly summarises how you have listened to their interest and needs, had them prioritise these for you and probed further to understand and quantify the impact of these being met. You have shown them a solution which meets all of the important aspects, explained how and why this is the case with your presentation, and subsequently illustrated how this will positively impact their particular situation.

To confidently make these types of statements or propositions, it's necessary to go through some form of questioning as we described earlier. In addition to presenting your solution, you will also quantify what impact it will have, ideally both operationally and financially. This approach not only reassures your customer of their wise decision, but also provides them with a solid rationale and supportive evidence to justify that decision.

Many times salespeople believe they have successfully convinced their client that their proposed solution will fit their needs only to be disappointed when there is no sale, or when the customer buys from the competition.

When we discussed decision making units (DMUs) earlier in the book we stressed the importance of really understanding how a decision is to be made. Regardless of what we will have been told, at some point some even more senior or influential person (they may not be the same thing) may get involved in approving an order, particularly one that is of a substantial value to the customer and therefore probably even more important to you and your business.

The usefulness therefore, of developing a **Differentiating Value Proposition or Statement** and having this in a format that can be used by your customer to support your proposal inside their business to their colleagues and/or boss, cannot be underestimated.

Many businesses, perhaps yours included, have invested in tools that can be used to generate such proposition or statements. These may include detailed financial projections, waterfall graphs, multiple slides and other written materials that can be shared inside the customer's business to support your proposed solution.

If you have these at your disposal, then use them, but remember the importance of a fully detailed questioning process, such as we describe in this book. This process will ensure you capture every important interest or need, prioritise these effectively and quantify the impact appropriately.

If you do not have such a tool available to use, don't despair. In our experience a version of these statements can be developed as a result of identifying the ways in which customer impact can be quantified and, working with your customer to develop or estimate these if necessary, enable a simple statement to be produced, put into writing after your meeting and included with any subsequent detailed proposal or follow up message.

In summary, the combination of the structured sales process and a compelling **Differentiating Value Proposition or Statement** provide you with a massively increased chance of success.

So, back to closing.

The key elements, as with all opportunities to close, are:

1. **Recognise the buying signals, either in words or via body language**

2. **Summarise the accepted benefits, built around verified and prioritised INs**

3. **Restate the value your proposal will add, providing a Differentiating Value Proposition or Statement using Make Money, Save Money, Feel Good to guide you**

4. **Ask for a commitment to progress, using a question or statement you feel comfortable with**

You may need to go through this process several times before you get the customer persuaded of the value of your product and this may take some tenacity on your part. The option to withdraw, or defer until a later time, and return with their permission when/if you are able to change your proposal to make it more acceptable to them is always there.

However, your successful closing rate will improve significantly if you adopt the process we explain and represent in the below drawing:

Respond and Close

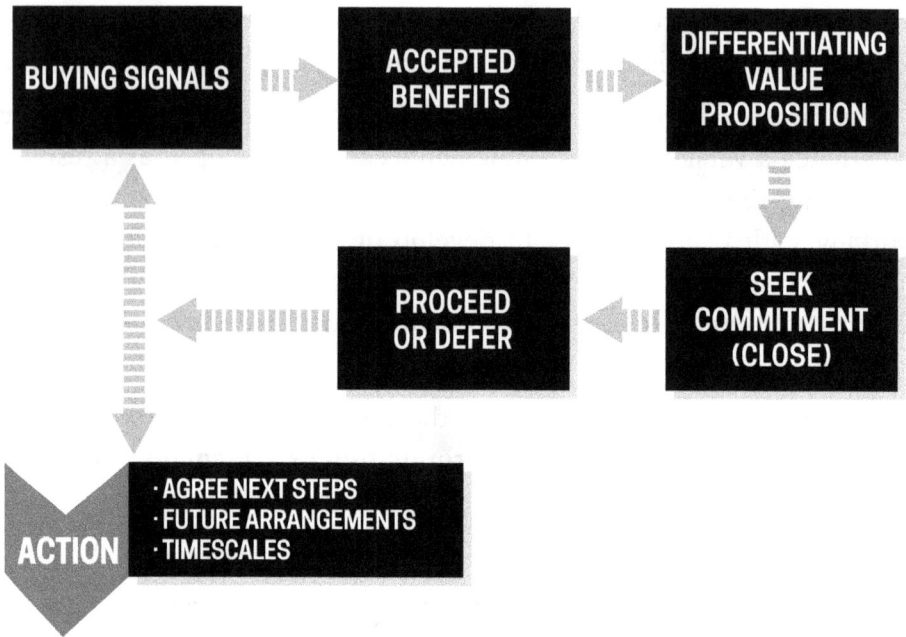

CHAPTER TWENTY - TWO

Call To Action

ACTION
· AGREE NEXT STEPS
· FUTURE ARRANGEMENTS
· TIMESCALES

This is the final stage of the sales process and/or call/visit when, having gained commitment to progress and possibly place an order, raise a specification or agree a contract, you ensure that there is agreement about what happens next, who is going to do what, and over what timescale.

We have observed on many occasions, when after a salesperson has obtained a commitment from a customer that, frequently as they're getting ready to leave, they feel the need to continue 'selling' by perhaps discussing how another customer really gained benefit from or appreciated a particular feature, that for this customer may not be important. This can lead to the customer pausing, reflecting on what has just been said, and as a result, either changing their mind or significantly elongating the process.

It is vital therefore that you or, as we have also observed, those who may be accompanying you, do not inadvertently, accidentally or unintentionally re-open the sales discussions by starting to discuss the various merits of the product or solution. It is time to move on.

Therefore, a simple plan of action that you make a written note of, and subsequently send via email to confirm, will be of immense value at this stage. The customer may of course offer to do this, in which case it is suggested you ensure that the key elements are noted while you are with the customer, and that you keep a written record of these.

A simple plan that contains basics such as those laid out, for example only, below will suffice:

No.	Agreed Action	By Whom	By When
1.	Send written confirmation of all agreed specifications to (customer name)	Salesperson Name	1 week
2.	Check all details are correct and initiate purchase process	Customer Name	2 weeks
3.	Confirm receipt of purchase order	Salesperson Name	2.5 weeks
4.	Confirm delivery date(s)	Salesperson Name	3 weeks
5.	1 month before due date, confirm all preparations to receive items are in place	Customer Name	1 month before delivery
6.	Confirm final Factory Acceptance Tests (FATs), User Acceptance Tests (UATs) or other trials as needed or appropriate and delivery date	Salesperson Name	As needed

This approach also gives you 'permission' to follow up with the customer if their actions are taking longer than agreed – you then avoid the potential 'silence' that precedes delay or even rejection.

It is also good practice to ensure that either the customer 'socialises' the intent to place the order or agrees to put you in contact with whomever else at his company he thinks it would be useful for you to know. Alternatively, they may be able to recommend you to another contact they have in their industry that is at a different company.

Therefore, asking the question such as:

"Mr. Customer, besides yourself, who else in your company might it be important that I meet with?"

Or

"Mr. Customer, besides yourself, who else do you know that might be interested in discussing our kinds of products and services?"

Asking this type of question, especially at this late stage in the process, will potentially identify new contacts or opportunities and is always worthwhile.

Depending on the response, it is also suggested that you also ask something such as:

"Do you mind if I mention your name to them when I call?"

Or

"Would you mind mentioning to them that we've spoken and that I'll look to contact them soon?"

This will also help to secure further appointments with potential customers in the future and in our experience is the most effective way to build out your contact base and maximise your face to face selling time.

Finally

Thank the customer for their time, commitment to the agreed actions and of course for their business and leave.

Is it time to celebrate?

Not yet, at least not too enthusiastically or openly especially while you are still on the customer's premises, including while sitting in their reception or in their car park. If your customer contact, or a colleague of theirs, observes you laughing and joking, fist pumping or high fiving, they may interpret this incorrectly. Be polite, happy, friendly, and respectful but leave the celebrations to a more appropriate place and time such as your office after the order has been closed. A business owner/manager, or finance colleague, will probably add that the appropriate time for celebration is when you have been paid by the customer.

Notwithstanding the above, this is a time to feel good about what you've been able to achieve as a result of your efforts and these feelings of exhilaration are a big part of why we enjoy being in sales.

CHAPTER TWENTY - THREE

Summary

```
┌─────────────┐   ┌─────────────┐   ┌─────────────┐   ┌─────────────┐   ┌─────────────┐   ┌─────────────┐
│ SITUATIONAL │   │  THE "BIG"  │   │  INTERESTS  │   │  CUSTOMER   │   │   PRESENT   │   │  CALL TO    │
│  QUESTIONS  │⇢⇢│  QUESTION   │⇢⇢│   & NEEDS   │⇢⇢│   IMPACT    │⇢⇢│  SOLUTION   │⇢⇢│   ACTION    │
└─────────────┘   └─────────────┘   └─────────────┘   └─────────────┘   └─────────────┘   └─────────────┘
```

| FEAR | ⇠ | FORCE PRICE OBJECTION | ⇠ | COMFORT |

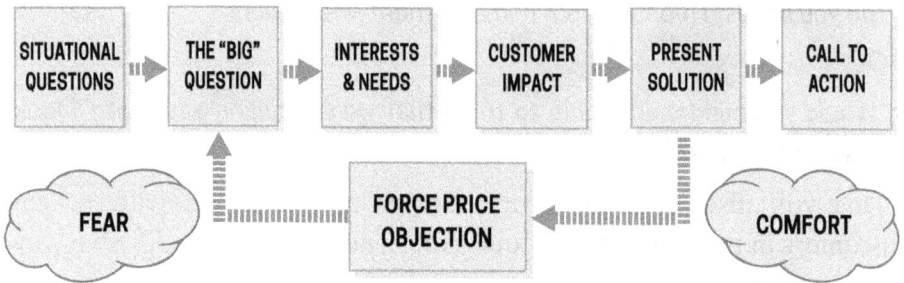

THE BIG FOUR INTERESTS & NEEDS

1	**2**	**3**	**4**
PRODUCT & SERVICE	LOGISTICS	COMMERCIAL	PERSONALISED SERVICES

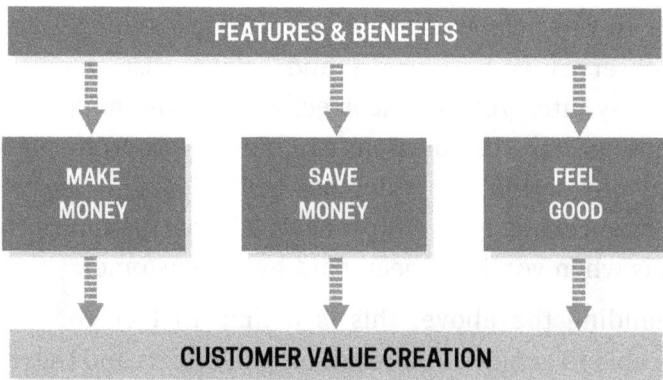

FEATURES & BENEFITS

MAKE MONEY	SAVE MONEY	FEEL GOOD

CUSTOMER VALUE CREATION

W hile this seeks to portray the complete process, start by developing your questioning skills. In our experience the most successful salespeople are those who develop the habit of asking the right questions, i.e. they are inherently curious or display a high level of capability to be curiously investigative. This, in our view, is the most important sales competency, as we explain further soon.

As you start to implement the skills and use this structure, we suggest you use the above diagram as a guide, to help you progress through each stage. Start by your preparation of potential questions, ask those that are relevant and then listen carefully.

A wise senior salesperson used to say:

"A customer doesn't care how much you know, until they know how much you care."

They only **know** you care when you ask them questions, listen actively and respond appropriately. The structured sales process is an enabler of this.

As you become more comfortable with the process, the sequence will flow more naturally, feel, from a customer's perspective, like any interesting conversation that they have and deliver value-generating opportunities for you, and most importantly for them too.

Try this on your next customer visit. You will be pleasantly surprised at how much more involved your customer will become, and how they will appreciate your taking an interest in their situation.

CHAPTER TWENTY - FOUR

Multi-Stage Complex Sales Situations

These are situations that will require you to plan your approach thoroughly, probably include the support from some of your colleagues on several occasions, need a number of face to face meetings, over a time-frame of at least several weeks or months, with many customer contacts, possibly located at different sites or even in different countries.

They are also likely to be of significant value to your customer and therefore undoubtedly of importance to your sales performance and business.

Invariably these involve multiple decision-makers (or a DMU), with varying priorities, perspectives and Interests and Needs that require satisfying. The importance of early clarification of this DMU, their priorities regarding INs, together with accepted methods of evaluating the impact of these being satisfied, is crucial to enable your successfully achieving a sale.

Within this book, we are not seeking to provide a detailed process for these situations, but as with the re-engaging process outlined previously, we reassert the importance of continually verifying INs, their impact and ensuring that, via appropriate presentations, you maintain a positive momentum.

The structured sales process incorporating the elements explained in this book, combined with effective re-engagement methods will be extremely powerful in these situations.

CHAPTER TWENTY - FIVE

Delivering Proposals

As a result of your successful meeting with a customer and using the structured sales process to good effect, there will be a time when a detailed proposal, that could be used by them to raise a purchase order with your company, will be required.

We suggest that you arrange to meet the customer to review this with them and leave behind a hard-copy version, possibly sending a digital version subsequently if required.

Using the approach similar to that we suggested when re-engaging, then summarising your prior discussions, concluding with the Differentiating Value Proposition or Statement and then explaining how your proposal meets this, will be the most effective way for you to ensure that all their requirements are met, and that you can conclude the sale with an agreement to raise a purchase order as soon as possible thereafter.

Depending on your products or services, your proposal may be extremely detailed, and run to several pages. In our experience such proposals that use a Differentiating Value Proposition or Statement in the opening page, moves directly to the substantive detail to include pricing, and then re-summarises the Differentiating Value Proposition or Statement, are the most effective.

Regardless, 'walking' your customer through it, ensuring that all their requirements are satisfied and agreeing next steps, ideally the placing of a purchasing order, significantly increase the success rate. In our experience, far too many opportunities have been lost as a result of sending the proposal, or having someone else send it, then failing to follow-up. Remember, your competitor may also be submitting a proposal and, if they follow-up while you do not, momentum may change and so could a decision you believed would be in your favour. Do not be the "we lost it on price" salesperson.

In this book, we explain the structured sales process in detail and, for ease of understanding, typically refer to 'a' solution. Implying there will be only one of these. The challenge with this single solution approach is that it effectively becomes what we describe as a "take it, or leave it" choice for the customer.

Increasing your chances of success by offering a range of solutions, but not so many that your customer becomes confused by the merits or shortcomings of these, will enable you to offer an "either (this solution) or (that solution)" choice for your customer. This situation results in a significant increase in success rates for salespeople compared with the "take it, or leave it" approach of a single solution, and is therefore encouraged.

Knowledge of your customer's situation, their budget, it's flexibility, your products and services and how these could be applied to best support your customer's 'make money', save money' and 'feel good' objectives will enable you to develop the appropriate number of solutions in any given scenario.

CHAPTER TWENTY - SIX

Relationships

We recognise and agree with many other sales leaders that establishing solid relationships is especially important to support your long-term effectiveness as a salesperson. These, as with almost any other relationship, should be built on mutual trust and understanding. The process of questioning explained in this book will support this by enabling you to demonstrate how interested in the customer you are.

It is also important to ask yourself, "What am I getting from this (customer) relationship?"

As a minimum we suggest you should be getting advance information on potential opportunities for your products and services, guidance through the customer's evaluation and procurement process, and ideally, what we describe as, the 'last look' before any decision is made on an opportunity that you have submitted a proposal for. By this we mean that you are kept informed, within the boundaries of relevant confidentiality, how your proposal is being thought of and how it compares with others being considered.

When a supportive customer relationship is coupled with strong sales skills and the use of a structured process, such as the one we focus on in this book, it will likely be a winning combination. The relationship will help you to understand the multiple influences and influencers within a customer organisation and, in particular, ensure you remain prepared to address issues ahead of them being expressed.

There are two examples of sales experiences we know intimately and use to illustrate the importance of relationships. Both situations were selling a new concept built around a mature product, that was not previously used by either customer in the manner proposed. They were complex sales situations, involving many influencers, across several of the different customer's functional areas, who were located at several sites. Both examples were successful for many reasons, the structured sales process was used to great effect, but without a doubt the salesperson's ability to build relationships was instrumental in ensuring the sales processes maintained momentum and were brought to successful conclusions.

Energy Company

A major global energy company had used the salesperson's products for several decades in a specific and limited set of applications, and were readily accepting of its merits. However, a significant opportunity to expand its use into other, more demanding application areas existed. Despite several attempts by various salespeople in many of the company's locations, no major acceptance and adoption of the product in this application had taken place.

This particular salesperson met an engineer who, it transpired, was a key influencer across his company. The salesperson used the structured sales method with this individual who became convinced of the operational and financial merits of the proposed solution, which was fundamentally a new approach to using the salesperson's product.

In order to gain acceptance and permission for it's use, it was necessary to gain the approval of a 'standards committee', which was in effect a component of the customer's Decision Making Unit (DMU) which also included finance, procurement, safety, operations and general management personnel. Many of these customer personnel were located in different sites and the challenge was to gain access to all these people, in a timely manner, to present a sound and well supported supported business case, to enable therefore the salesperson's product to be accepted in this demanding application.

The relationship with the engineer, who was extremely well respected within his company, and was destined for senior management, became crucial. He was able to navigate the customer's internal organisation over a six-month period to arrange multiple meetings, presentations and discussions that culminated in the product being approved for use in this, significantly expanded, set of applications.

Subsequently this resulted in multiple orders for products, training, and installation equipment that previously would not have occurred. A three-fold increase in sales for these products was achieved with this customer during the following year with continued growth thereafter.

The structured sales process identified multiple opportunities for the customer to save money on installation time, make money by reducing operational downtime and feel good by reducing hazardous operations while maintaining safety standards.

However, it was undoubtedly the relationship built by the salesperson with the engineer that enabled the sales process to reach across the customer organisation. There were many internal resistors to change and the engineer was able to effectively 'coach' the salesperson to ensure that at the many meetings, some in a group format with ten to fifteen customer personnel, others involving fewer people, the likely concerns were addressed by the salesperson using appropriate and prepared evidence, to ensure these concerns were fully addressed and overcome.

A great example of ensuring a relationship made a positive impact!

Equipment Manufacturing Company

This situation involved one of the world's leading engineering brands and its power generation equipment.

This division of the customer, was aware of the salesperson's product but had never seriously considered it for use as it was perceived, by them, to be too expensive. There was a four-fold increase in the purchase price of equivalent products to be overcome in order to convince the customer of the merits and, while several attempts had been made, none had been successful due to this significant price obstacle.

At an industry forum the salesperson met the senior executive officer of the company, who had been a keynote speaker. During a number of discussions over lunch, and at several breaks, the salesperson was able to learn from the customer that they had begun to experience significant equipment failures within their own global customer base. This was causing them considerable 'pain' due to emergency maintenance visits and product repairs, carried out at their cost, within their warranty period. In addition, and most importantly, this situation was negatively impacting their brand.

The salesperson explained, in principle, using a form of 'elevator pitch' why he believed his product may be of interest to the customer, and an agreement to meet the following week was reached.

In order to prepare for the meeting, the salesperson consulted with his colleagues, including senior technical and application personnel, and collated some evidence to enable the anticipated concerns to be addressed.

The meeting took place and went very well, with the salesperson using the structured sales process to build upon the knowledge gained during their initial meeting at the forum. He developed a solid understanding of the customer's requirements, their decision-making process, including the key influencers whose support would be needed.

The positive impact of a resolution of the customer's existing challenges was developed with the customer, and quantified, operationally and financially. It was agreed that removal of their 'pain' would certainly result in the customer saving money on product warranty claims, feeling good as a result of improved customer relations and reverse the slide in their brand reputation. The four-fold increase in initial purchase price of the replacement equipment was agreed to be minimal in comparison with the positive impact described, and would in reality enable the customer to make money as a result.

A presentation of the salesperson's product took place, with the customer enthusiastically concluding that he would 'get his people' aligned in order to begin using it.

As with the example of the energy company, there were several influencers in key positions who, despite being in more junior roles to the senior executive officer, nonetheless needed to be convinced so that they would support the transition to the 'new' product offered by the salesperson.

A period of testing, evaluation and review involving the product design, manufacturing, marketing, sales, finance and procurement functions took place over a six-month period. The relationship with the senior executive officer undoubtedly ensured the momentum was maintained and finally a confirmation of acceptance was achieved.

This resulted in a complete transition to the salesperson's product being phased in by the customer and resulting in new sales of circa $1m annually.

As with the prior example, the structured sales process was successfully applied here too, but again the relationship with the senior executive was pivotal, as without this it is doubtful the customer would have maintained the momentum needed to eventually adopt the salesperson's solution.

There are many other examples where a great customer relationship has assisted salespeople, but when this relationship is used effectively, and in conjunction with the structured sales process, seemingly impossible challenges can be overcome!

An understandable question therefore is:

"How do I build effective relationships with my customers?"

As previously mentioned, any meaningful relationship should benefit all involved and be built upon a solid foundation of mutual trust, respect and understanding.

We can only achieve this if we, as the salesperson, take a genuine interest in our customers by practising the approaches to questioning, active listening, respectfully challenging assertions and proposing solutions that meet the needs we have taken the time to identify, verify and prioritise. Demonstrating that you take sufficient time, energy and patience to fully understand their 'world' and the implications of improving this, in whatever manner your solutions can, will be noticed and in most cases appreciated.

Additionally, fundamentals such as being polite, punctual, prepared, honest, following through on commitments, while being considerate of the customer's potentially changing circumstances, are essential in establishing the long-term respect necessary to develop the strong customer relationships we all desire.

CHAPTER TWENTY-SEVEN

Sales Competencies

As a result of working with many salespeople, we have observed habits, or behaviours, that significantly jeopardized their performance and effectiveness. Here are a couple of examples.

I. Some salespeople believe the customer will buy from them out of loyalty or obligation. On so many occasions this results in lost orders and opportunities, frequently explained by the salesperson as having been "lost on price". In reality, this was probably not lost on price, but lost because the salesperson did not understand the customer's decision-making procedure, buying process, or other key aspect, such as any competitors being considered. An effective questioning process at the outset would have avoided this.

II. We have also observed, that even when a salesperson has been trained how to deploy a structured sales process, they choose not to and explain "that was not a suitable visit to use my sales skills". In our opinion, every visit is an opportunity to deploy some element of these skills.

The above examples, and coaching salespeople to avoid them, has evolved into a significant body of work undertaken several times with differing companies, selling varied products and services into broadly differing markets and across multiple geographies.

This work involved engaging professional psychologists to observe salespeople in their roles, identifying the competencies being displayed, verifying these with their management teams and ultimately collating these into a structure we call a 'competency framework'.

Competencies are the observable application of behaviours, knowledge, skills, and personal characteristics that enable superior job performance.

They are the factors that will drive exceptional performance, differentiate you in the marketplace, and enable your continued growth and success.

Of these competencies, the top four or five observable behavioural competencies can vary depending on the person, their company, their products and services together with the markets, sectors, and types of customer they are selling into.

However, consistently the most important competency to focus on has been, and remains, that of 'Curious Investigation.' We are therefore including an extract from the framework we have developed over the page.

If a sales person becomes accomplished in their questioning skills, combined with their active listening and other communication skills, their track record of success is materially improved when compared with those who routinely start a sales presentation without having asked the types of questions we've outlined in this book – typically because they believe the customer expects them (the salesperson) to already know all of this information. Not taking the time to go through this questioning process invariably leads to misunderstandings, multiple objections and delayed or lost sales opportunities.

Further detail on this, the broader framework of many other sales related competencies and the varied way they can be used to help assess capabilities, identify opportunities for development and support a sales coaching process, can be found in the accompanying book on 'Professional Sales Leadership and Management', due for release in 2021.

Below is a definition of the most important competency a successful sales person will possess and continually develop. Also shown are some examples of the positively or negatively observable behaviours.

Ask yourself;
- **How many of these behaviours listed below apply to you?**
- **What can I do to increase the positive?**
- **How do I reduce the negative?**

Curious Investigation

Definition: Is future-focused, inquisitive, and open-minded; seeks out evolving and innovative ways to add value to their company and their customers.

Positive Indicators

✔	Frequently and appropriately asks 'Why?', 'Why Not?' or 'For What Reasons?'
✔	Explores product and brand developments to understand their features and functions and how they can add value to customers
✔	Conducts insight interviews with customers and identifies issues that cost the customer money
✔	Obtains first-hand customer feedback and uses it for improvements in products and services
✔	Understands the customer environment and the ways in which your company's services and products can add value in that environment.
✔	Generate and use insights that help customer better manage their business
✔	Probe to uncover and validate customer interests and needs (INs) – both stated and implicit
✔	Probe current methods to identify gaps and potential differentiators
✔	Develops understanding of how and by whom decisions are made in the customer environment
✔	Gains insight into customer perspective, including potential objections to the proposed sales solution, customer preferences, and expected results from the solution
✔	Observes the customer's premises for signs of competitors products and unnecessarily negative current impact for their customer
✔	Finds different means of developing business with a customer
✔	Is opportunistic – in response to a CON sees an opportunity for either a new way of doing things or another way of a customer viewing things
✔	Finds ways to engage a customer currently supplied by a competitor
✔	Quickly identifies where business opportunities are with both existing and new customers

Negative indicators

✗	Does not know or identify who the key decision makers are
✗	Does not identify the full potential for the product/service/technology
✗	Does not seek to develop a full understanding of their products, services, markets, applications, and customers
✗	Completes a scant fact find

Be honest with yourself, better still, ask someone you work with and trust who has observed you selling, to help you identify those behaviours that you routinely demonstrate. Then, reflect on this and consider what you can choose to do differently that will develop this competency. For most of us, a few subtle changes can have a significantly positive impact our behaviours and enhance our abilities as related to this competency.

CHAPTER TWENTY - EIGHT

Objectives of the Book for Readers

HOW DID WE DO?

During Reading

1. Introduce a structured sales process to readers and provide them with opportunities to customise it to their situation.

2. Introduce the competency of Curious Investigation, explain its relevance and applicability to sales and suggest methodologies to enhance this.

3. Instill readers with a desire to enthusiastically put the process and tools introduced and explained into use in their daily selling activities.

Within Three-Months of Reading

1. Develop and enhance through practice a structured, consistent sales methodology

2. Improve your opportunity conversion rate, however they may be generated, and increase your sales.

3. Understand how you can better utilise all existing business tools and processes such as your CRM and quote generator/configurator to gain

personal and collective benefit from them.

4. Enjoy your sales role more as a result of feeling more confident in every sales situation and increasing your earnings.

One Year After Reading

1. Remain stimulated and equipped to meet and exceed your sales objectives or targets consistently.

2. Produce improved standards of personal performance and income for the remainder of your career in sales.

3. Share with enthusiasm your sales skills and love of sales as a career.

How did you do with your objectives?

a. On completion of reading

b. Three months after reading

c. One year after reading

CHAPTER TWENTY - NINE

Final Thoughts

Sales is a profession, so why not become the most rounded, competent, skilled professional you can?

Defining and quantifying the attributable value a solution contributes to a business has become of primary importance across all markets and geographies. Salespeople need to master the process, skills, tools, techniques and behaviours that enable this, so that they become, and remain, successful.

The ideas, concepts, methods and exercises included in this book will, if implemented, enable you to build a successful career in sales.

The final observation we make is that in order to start using the ideas explained in this book it is highly likely you will be trying something that you are not familiar with.

This takes courage.

Recognise this for what it is, draw upon your inner confidence and try it.

Start with preparing your questions, think about your customer's likely responses and how you will in-turn respond, work with colleagues to role-play if possible but most importantly have the courage to try it – this approach works, and you can have fun with it too.

Remember:

Effective selling involves asking a customer, who either is or you hope will become, your friend a question, giving them the courtesy of listening to their answer, probing to fully understand their needs, offering them a solution that meets these and asking them to buy it from you.

In the words of Frank Dick OBE, a successful athletics coach who has trained many Olympic medalists:

If not you – who?

If not now – when?

Practise, practise, practise!

APPENDIX

Glossary of terms / abbreviations:

Big Question – a question intended to uncover the Interests and Needs of a customer

Big Four INs – Describe what the Product & Service, Logistic, Commercial and Personalised Service requirements are from the customer's perspective

INs – Interests and needs

CONs – Concerns, Obstacles and Negatives

DMU – Decision Making Unit

GDP – Gross Domestic Product

PMI – Purchasing Manager's Index

CRM – Customer (or client) Relationship Manager

Acknowledgements

Mike Cairns, Sales Director, Ishida Europe – for his continuous enthusiasm for sales, sales leadership and the development of people and their ideas

Rody Salas, President RSR International – for his endless support, coaching, mentoring, ideas, development of sales strategies, wisdom, creation of the "make money, save money, feel good" statement and positivity.

John Dare, formerly of Swagelok's Bristol based distributorship – for having the confidence in my potential to offer me my first sales, and subsequently sales management, roles, shaping my early career and reinforcing personal values that remain key to me. Rest in peace John, fondest memories and greatest respect for a true gentleman.

Bob Aldridge, formerly of Swagelok Company – for the inspirational combination of sales skills, humour, and wisdom. Rest in peace Bob, fondest memories.

Isabelle Perrett, HR Director – for her intelligent application of people development processes

Swagelok Company and their distributors, SPX Flow, SPX Corporation and their distributors, the team at Ishida Europe – all for providing me with multiple learning opportunities and experiences, many of which are reflected here too.

All salespeople, sales leaders and customers I have ever worked with from many companies – for providing me with multiple learning opportunities and experiences, many of which have found their way into this book.

My wife Clare, sister Stella and step-daughter Becky - for their support, proof reading and honest feedback.

Andy Spencer and the team at Engedi Group

Useful further reading options / suggestions:

Seven Habits of Highly Effective People – Stephen Covey

The Goal – Eliyahu M. Goldratt & Jeff Cox

Let's Get Real or Let's Not Play: Transforming the Buyer/Seller Relationship - Mahan Khalsa and Randy Illig

How to Master the Art of Selling – Tom Hopkins

www.ingramcontent.com/pod-product-compliance
Lightning Source LLC
Chambersburg PA
CBHW071159200326
41519CB00018B/5289